# THE DRONE PILOT HANDBOOK

## First Edition

### Everything You Need to Know to Pass the Part 107 Exam and Fly Drones Commercially

**By Zac Elliott**
**Creator of TheLegalDrone.com**

All versions of this book are dedicated to my wife, Emily. Without her trust and support for some of my crazy ideas, this book wouldn't exist.

Her support has been instrumental in all of my endeavors.

This is a disclaimer. I am not providing you with legal advice. Rather, this book is for informational purposes only. If you need legal advice, you should speak with a licensed attorney. Nothing contained in this book is intended to substitute for legal advice from a qualified, licensed attorney that can advise you regarding your specific situation. Even if you complete any of contact form or are involved in any e-mail correspondence or courses, no attorney-client relationship has been formed. You agree to complete your own due diligence and make a decision on attorney representation exclusively on your own.

# TABLE OF CONTENTS

# INTRODUCTION

By the end of this book, you will be armed with the information you need to achieve a passing score on the FAA Part 107 knowledge exam. This book will provide you with:
- In-depth chapters about each of the subject areas on the test;
- Bonus content such as study guides, infographics and cram sheets;
- Sample test questions at the end of each chapter; and
- Two full length (60 question) practice tests

# WHAT WILL WE STUDY?

The Part 107 test is broken down into five overarching topics. The percentages listed out from each topic represents roughly the number of test questions that will be pulled from each topic.

- **Regulations (15-25%)**

  o This chapter covers Part 107 generally, requirements to get your remote pilot certificate, where you can and can't fly, what you are required to have with you when flying, and getting Part 107 waivers and authorizations.

- **Airspace (15-25%)**

  o This chapter discusses classes of airspace surrounding airports (Classes B, C, D and E) as well as uncontrolled airspace (Class G). We will also discuss airspace restrictions such as temporary flight restrictions and warning areas.

- **Operations (35-45%)**

  o This chapter flows well from the previous section on airspace. An important part of understanding airspace is how to recognize each type of airspace on a sectional chart. So this chapter deals more with aeronautical charts, types of airports, sources of airport information as well as latitude and longitude.

- **Weather (11-16%)**

  o In this chapter, we will discuss aviation weather tools such as METARS, PIREPS and SIGMETS. After reading this chapter, uou will be able to read these weather tools and determine whether it is safe to fly in current or forecasted weather. Additionally, we will discuss basic weather concepts and how you can recognize the formation of bad weather using the aviation weather tools.

- **Loading and Performance (7-11%)**

  o This chapter deals with a myriad of topics and tends to be kind of a catch-all. It will discuss weight, stability and other load factors as well as emergency procedures, crew resource management, radio communication procedures, physiological factors in pilot performance as well as aeronautical decision-making and judgment.

This book will be broken down into chapters based upon each of these topics and will have practice questions at the end of each chapter. The focus here is to provide you with the knowledge that you need to pass the Part 107 knowledge exam. Thus, the chapters will focus as much as possible on the concepts as they relate to the Part 107 drone pilot.

After the chapters on the test topics, I've also included a few chapters on relevant information for the licensed commercial drone pilot. This includes Part 107 test taking tips, drone registration, and getting waiver and authorizations using LAANC and the drone zone. The final chapters in this book are two full length practice tests with answer keys.

This chapter of the book is going to introduce the Part 107 regulations, including pilot and aircraft requirements as well as general operating rules for Part 107 commercial drone pilots.

## PART 107 – GENERAL OVERVIEW

In June of 2016, the FAA began regulating flying small unmanned aerial systems (which are technically called "sUAS" but I will call drones throughout this book) commercially using Part 107. Prior to this, the FAA had used something called a 333 exemption, which was more difficult to obtain than a Part 107 license. Although it was an initial step was in the right direction, it was very inefficient and it quickly became clear that this highly manual process was not accomplishing its goals.

The new Part 107 regulations rolled out in June of 2016 were meant to deal with this backlog and have continued to evolve into a much more automated system. This allowed drone pilots to get licensed much easier and fly in numerous situations that were previously unregulated (and possibly unsafe) once they became licensed.

### PILOT REQUIREMENTS:

In order to become licensed under Part 107, a pilot must:

- be at least 16 years old;
- pass an initial aeronautical knowledge test at an FAA-approved knowledge testing center (which is what you're currently studying for;
- be vetted by the Transportation Safety Administration (TSA).

**Important note for applicants that already have a traditional or manned pilot's license:**

If you already hold a Part 61 pilot's certificate and have completed a flight review within the past 24 months, you are able to complete your Part 107 training online.

## AIRCRAFT REQUIREMENTS:

Under Part 107 your drone must:

- Weigh less than 55 lbs;

- Be registered if it weighs more than .55 pounds no matter if you intend to use it recreationally or commercially.

**Potential test question**

Remember the exact phrasing regarding the upper limits on weight, as this is frequently a test question.

## OPERATING RULES:

Under Part 107, the following general rules apply to all drone flights. A commercial drone pilot:
- Can fly in Class G airspace
- Must keep the aircraft in sight (visual line-of-sight)
- Must fly under 400 feet
- Must fly during the day
- Must fly at or below 100 mph
- Must yield right of way to manned aircraft
- Must NOT fly over people
- Must NOT fly from a moving vehicle

Although these are general rules, as a licensed commercial drone pilot, you do have the ability to request waivers and/or authorizations regarding each of these requirements. Although this process is undergoing changes at the moment (the introduction of immediate airspace authorizations via the LAANC system), each of these requirements can be waived through a successful application to the FAA.

## PART 107 – REMOTE PILOT CERTIFICATE & APPLICATION PROCESS

The Part 107 application process actually isn't that bad, but there are a few hoops that you will initially need to jump through. The good news is that once you have your license, renewal is A LOT easier.

## PILOT CERTIFICATE REQUIREMENTS

- Certificate must be easily accessible by the remote pilot during all UAS operations;
- Certificate is valid for two years and all certificate holders must pass a recurrent knowledge test every two years.

## APPLICATION PROCESS FOR NEW APPLICANTS

- Schedule an appointment with a Knowledge Testing Center. You will set up your exam through an organization called PSI and they will schedule your exam with a local office that you choose while on the phone with them.
- Pass the knowledge test.
- Fill out FAA Form 8710-13 using the FAA's online Integrated Airman Certificate and/or Rating Application system (IACRA).
    - o This will require you to register on the IACRA system.
    - o Login with your username and password
    - o Click "Start New Application" follow the prompts accordingly.
- After a TSA background check, you will receive a confirmation e-mail, which should include instructions for printing out your temporary pilot certificate.
- A permanent remote pilot certificate will be sent to you via regular mail. It will look a lot like a manned pilot's license.

## COST AND EXPIRATION

- Knowledge Testing Centers charge $150 to people seeking to take their aeronautical knowledge test.
- You will be required to pass a recurrent aeronautical knowledge test every 24 months in order to keep your remote pilot certificate current.

## APPLICATION PROCESS FOR RENEWAL OF PART 107 LICENSE

The application process for someone looking to renew their Part 107 license is pretty simplified. You don't need to fill out any IACRA forms or get another TSA background check. Another good thing is that the test itself is a bit abbreviated. Instead of 60 questions, you only have to take a test with 40 questions. The information on the test is also abbreviated, where you do not need to know weather or loading & performance information again. Check out Chapter 9, which includes a full section on the renewal exam. You will, however, be required to pay the same $150 fee to take the test again. Who doesn't love paying to take a test?

Also, after you pass the renewal test, the test facility will provide you with a piece of paper showing your information (and indicating that you passed) and at least one copy of this paper will be embossed with their seal. **It's really important that you keep this paper safe, because you will not be getting another license.** Instead, you will need to show this information along with your original license card if you are ever asked for your Part 107 license. The good news is you should get a second copy of this piece of paper, which you can keep with your drone gear. In addition, I also took a picture of mine and saved it in Evernote and Google Drive so that I'll always have it.

## PART 107 - FLIGHT OPERATIONS & WAIVERS

Next, we're going to discuss the rules for Part 107 operations of your drone and how to get Part 107 waivers. With your Remote Pilot Certification, the general rules are as follows.

**You CAN:**

> **Potential test question**
>
> Remember the exact phrasing regarding official sunset, as this is frequently a test question.

- Fly in Class G airspace without air traffic control (ATC) permission.
- Fly without a visual observer.
- Fly during the day.
- Fly during twilight (30 minutes before official sunset to 30 minutes after sunset local time) if you have appropriate anti-collision lighting.
- Carry an external load if it is securely attached to the UAS and does not adversely affect the flight characteristics of the UAS.
- Transport property for compensation or hire, so long as the entire UAS with payload is under 55 lbs.

**Scan the QR code to check out a helpful video test question to help you better understand flying a drone after official sunset.**

**You CANNOT**
- Fly in Class B, C, D, and E airspace without ATC permission.
- Fly your drone in a reckless manner.
- Fly beyond an unaided visual line of sight (VLOS) with the UAS.
- Fly using a first person viewer, such as goggles, unless you also have a visual observer.
- Fly more than one drone at a time.
- Fly at night without an FAA waiver.
- Fly in visibility of less than three miles from your control station.
- Fly beyond 400 feet above ground level unless you are within 400 feet of a structure.
- Fly faster than 100 mph.
- Fly over anyone who is not directly participating in the UAS operations, unless they are either under a covered structure or a non-moving vehicle.
- Fly from a moving vehicle unless you are flying over a sparsely populated area.

## OTHER REQUIREMENTS

- You must make your UAS available to the FAA for inspection or testing upon request and must provide any associated and required records under the rule. I've never been asked for this information (not even by local police) but those are the rules and honestly, having this information with you would be very helpful in the event that someone has questions about the legality of what you're doing.
- You must report any accident that results in serious injury, loss of consciousness, or property damage of at least $500 to the FAA within 10 days of the accident.

The FAA considers an injury to be a "serious injury" if it qualifies as a Level 3 injury or higher on the Abbreviated Injury Scale (AIS) of the Association for the Advancement of Automotive Medicine. The AIS system is an anatomical scoring system that ranks the severity of a given injury and is a standard that is widely used by emergency personnel. I realize this is a bit in the weeds, but as an attorney, I saw this definition and was curious how a "serious injury" was defined.

## PART 107 WAIVERS & AUTHORIZATIONS

The good news is that although there are a lot of rules on what you can and can't do under Part 107, the FAA also provides the ability to get waivers from those rules. Check out Chapter 10 which discusses getting Part 107 Waivers and Authorizations. When it comes to airspace authorization and waivers, the FAA has teamed up with several private companies to provide waivers services via online applications. The system used is called the LAANC system (because everything in aviation is *required* to have an acronym). LAANC stands for Low Altitude Authorization and Notification Capability. It just rolls right off of your tongue, doesn't it? I'm a huge fan of Kittyhawk and Airmap, both of which allow you to get instant approval where the FAA has rolled this system out and it has been adopted by the airport. At this point the LAANC system is live nationwide, but some airports have not yet begun to use it.

For other types of waivers, you still have to fill out an online application with the FAA through the Drone Zone portal, and approval can still take months. Because waivers aren't something that you will be tested on, I'm not going to get into the details about how exactly to get them here. Suffice it to say that it can be done. If you want more information, check out Chapter 10 on the specifics of getting waivers and authorizations.

**Question 1.** According to 14 CFR part 48, when must a person register a small UA with the Federal Aviation Administration?

    A. When the small UA is used for any purpose other than as a model aircraft.

    B. Only when the operator will be paid for commercial services.

    C. All civilian small UAs weighing greater than .55 pounds must be registered regardless of its intended use.

**Question 2.** To avoid a possible collision with a manned airplane, you estimate that your small UA climbed to an altitude greater than 600 feet AGL. To whom must you report the deviation?

    A. The FAA, upon request

    B. Air Traffic Control.

    C. The National Transportation Safety Board.

**Question 3.** You may operate an sUAS from a moving vehicle when no property is carried for compensation or hire

    A. Over a parade or other social events

    B. Over suburban areas

    C. Over a sparsely populated area

**Question 4.** The FAA may approve your application for a waiver of provisions in part 107 only when it has been determined that the proposed operation

    A. Can be safely conducted under the terms of that certificate of waiver

    B. Involves public aircraft or air carrier operations

    C. Will be conducted outside the United States

**Question 5.** According to 14 CFR part 107, an sUAS is an unmanned aircraft system weighing

A. 55 kg or less.
B. Less than 55 lbs.
C. 55 lbs or less.

**Question 1.**  C
**Question 2.**  A
**Question 3.**  C
**Question 4.**  A
**Question 5.**  B

Airspace is a heavily tested topic on the Part 107 exam. This makes sense because one of the most applicable things you will be doing as a commercial drone pilot is to fly in controlled airspace. And the FAA's main purpose is to keep the national airspace safe, so making sure Part 107 pilots understand airspace is a high priority on the test. This chapter will discuss airspace classifications as well as special use airspace and how to recognize all of it on a sectional chart. If you want more detail on how to read a sectional chart, Chapter 3 discusses this topic in depth.

## AIRSPACE CLASSIFICATIONS

For drone pilots, airspace classification can be really difficult, typically because the average drone pilot is someone who is unfamiliar with aviation to begin with. If you have not already, you will quickly become familiar with a flight planning map called a Visual Flight Rules (VFR) Sectional. Everyone just refers to these maps as sectionals. The sectional indicates airspace classifications along with a multitude of other helpful markers. All markings on the sectional are measured in height above mean sea level. To familiarize yourself with a sectional chart and its markings, your time will be best spent reviewing a sectional legend (just Google it). Another place to get sectionals to review and learn about individual markings is vfrmap.com. This will allow you to see any part of the United States and to become familiar with the map. Additionally though, it will ultimately be helpful to zoom in on your local area and get a better idea of the airports near you as well as determining their airspace, etc.

The best advice I can give you is to actually open a sectional in one browser window and a sectional legend in another window. Place them side by side and look at the markings. Chances are, after some practice, you will be able to identify most of them. I know the sectional chart will initially look pretty overwhelming, but that is just because of the amount of information that is contained in this one map. If there's something you're struggling with, feel free to contact me. My e-mail address is at the front of this book.

## CONTROLLED VS. UNCONTROLLED AIRSPACE

The key to airspace classification for drone pilots is to know that all airspace in the United States is either controlled or uncontrolled. Classes A, B, C, D, and E are controlled types of airspace. Class G is uncontrolled airspace. We will discuss each of these below except Class A because it is generally 18,000 MSL and above and really doesn't apply to what we're learning about here. If you're flying at 18,000 feet, you've got way cooler drones than I do and probably already have some pretty sick training on how to fly them.

To start out, just know that you will always need permission to fly in controlled airspace. Once you have your Part 107 license, you have permission to fly drones for commercial purposes in the U.S. in uncontrolled airspace (Class G) but will still need additional permission to fly in controlled airspace (everything else). Chapter 10 covers how to get waivers and authorizations.

## WHAT IS CLASS B AIRSPACE?

Class B airspace surrounds the nation's busiest airports (think B for busy) and is indicated by a solid blue line on a sectional. It looks a lot like a 3-tiered upside down wedding cake overtop of the airport. The smallest section of the cake is typically a 5-mile radius containing the main portion of the airspace from the surface to 10,000 ft MSL plus two outer shelves. Each outer shelf encompasses a larger swath of land but does not reach down to the surface. If you look at the figure below, the airspace surrounding CVG, you can see the markings on the map showing 100/21. On a sectional chart, the last two zeros of the altitude will be cut off, but this indicates that Class B airspace in this area extends from 2,100 feet MSL to 10,000 feet MSL. For our purposes here, we are mainly focused on the layer of the "cake" that extends to the ground because this is where you will be flying. Because the outer rings of the "cake" do not reach to the ground, you likely will never encounter a situation where you will be flying at that altitude.

If you look at the figure below, the airspace surrounding CVG (Cincinnati International Airport), you can see the markings on the map showing 100/SFC, 100/21, 100/35, and 100/50. I've added red squares over these markings on the image below, but please note that these markings are *not* usually covered in red on a sectional. I just did this to call your attention to it.

The last two zeros of the altitude will be cut off, but 100/21 indicates that Class B airspace in this area extends from 2,100 feet MSL to 10,000 feet MSL. It is the same reading with each of the rest of these notations. The top number indicates the top of the airspace and the bottom number indicates the floor of the airspace. SFC as the bottom "number" means surface, and is usually reserved for the top tier of the "wedding cake," which is the circle closest to the airport.

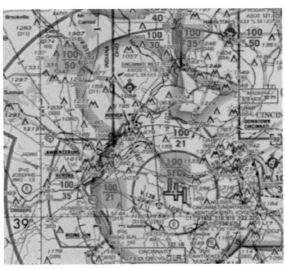

## WHAT IS CLASS C AIRSPACE?

Class C airspace is typically less busy than class B airspace and is indicated on a sectional by a solid magenta line. These airports still have a control tower. Like Class B airspace, Class C airspace also has an upper shelf (think upside down wedding cake again, only this time it is a 2-tiered cake). Class C only has one shelf instead of the two associated with class B. Class C airspace is usually from the surface to 4,000 MSL, which is again different than Class B in that it does not extend as high. Despite the fact that you will likely never be flying your drone at or above 4,000 MSL, this will be important information to know and understand for purposes of getting your license. Although the size and shape of Class C airspace can (and usually is) tailored to the specific airport, the bottom layer of the cake usually has a 5 nautical mile radius, just like Class B.

Below, you can see that the bottom later of the cake shows that Lexington, Kentucky's airport has Class C airspace extending from the surface up to 5,000 MSL. Note that this is a departure from the normal 4,000 foot MSL ceiling of typical Class C. The outer shelf extends from 2,200 feet MSL to 5,000 feet MSL. Additionally, the numbers in magenta (50/SFC and 50/22) indicate the floor and ceiling of the airspace just like Class B above.

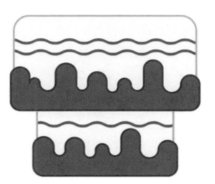

## WHAT IS CLASS D AIRSPACE

Class D airspace is typically surrounding an airport with a control tower, although it is yet again less busy than airports with Classes B and C airspace. It is indicated on a sectional chart by a dashed blue line. It typically extends from the surface to 2,500 feet MSL and is also tailored to the airport. Class D airspace is indicated by a dashed blue line on a sectional. Although you can also use the wedding cake analogy here, it would simply be a one layer cake, as Class D airspace does not have shelves like Classes B and C.

**Want to know how to deal with Class D airspace that has a part-time tower? Scan the QR code to check out the video test question.**

Below is Cincinnati, with its international airport, as discussed above, as well as Lunken airport off to the east. Within the dashed blue line surrounding Lunken Airport is the number 30 within four brackets, as seen here.

This indicates that the top of the Class D airspace is 3,000 feet MSL. Note that this is a departure from the normal top altitude for Class D airspace of 2,500 feet MSL.

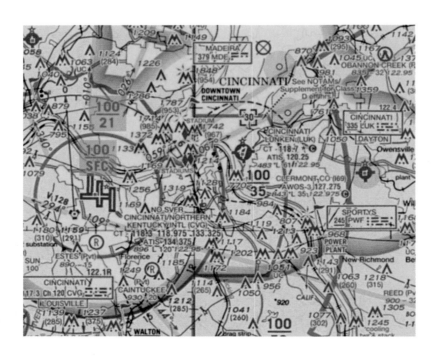

WHAT IS CLASS E AIRSPACE?

Class E airspace is the most common type of airspace in the United States but is easily misunderstood partly because it has two variations: Transitional and Enroute. Second, Class E airspace is measured in feet above ground level (AGL) instead of mean sea level (MSL) like all other airspace.

Transitional Class E airspace generally shows up around airports and is identified on a sectional as a faded magenta ring. This ring indicates that class E airspace begins at 700 feet AGL, extending upward. Additionally, sometimes airports with a faded magenta ring will also have a dashed magenta line around them. This indicates that Class E airspace extends down to the ground within this circle.

The picture below is a great example of both. Boone airport to the west is surrounded by Class E airspace that begins at 700 feet AGL because of the faded magenta ring. Ames airport to the east not only has Class E airspace from 700 feet above ground level within the faded magenta ring, but it *also* has Class E airspace to the ground within the dashed magenta circle.

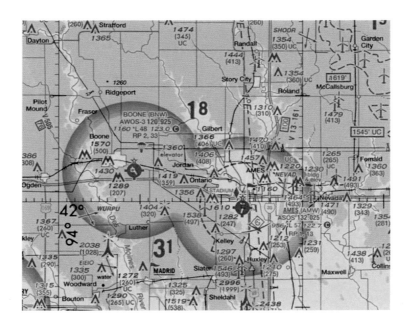

Enroute Class E airspace is from 1,200 ft AGL to 18,000 feet AGL and is not associated with airports. You should be familiar with Enroute Class E airspace for purposes of the test, but recognize that you will likely never be flying your drone at 1,200 feet AGL, and thus, will not need to worry about it when flying unmanned aircraft for commercial purposes.

To be clear, there are places where Class E airspace does not begin until 14,500 and these are typically understood on a sectional chart just by the absence of a Class E floor on the chart of 700 or 1,200 feet AGL. Finally, there is Class E airspace above 60,000 feet MSL, but again, this will not apply to you for purposes of the Part 107 exam.

## WHAT IS CLASS G AIRSPACE?

Remember how I said that the key to airspace classification for drone pilots is knowing what's controlled vs. uncontrolled? Class G airspace is the only form of uncontrolled airspace in the United States. Because it is uncontrolled, recognizing Class G airspace is different than recognizing any other airspace. It is not marked on a sectional, but instead can be understood as not being Classes A, B, C, D and E. We have not discussed Class A airspace, but this is unnecessary for purposes of the Part 107 knowledge exam because Class A airspace in the United States begins at 18,000 feet MSL and is not implicated in flying small unmanned aircraft. Remember, Class G airspace is uncontrolled, and once you have your Part 107 license, you are able to legally fly here without additional approval.

## SPECIAL USE AIRSPACE

Special use airspace is exactly what it sounds like: Airspace that is marked off for a specific and special type of use. Flying drones in special use airspace depends wholly on the type of special use airspace, which we will discuss below. Usually, it involves something that could be hazardous to air traffic, and other times it involves issues of national security. The FAA even has a "No Drone Zone" campaign that discusses flying drones in special use airspace. No matter what the special use, it is important to know if you can fly there legally.

## PROHIBITED AREAS

Prohibited areas are identified on a sectional by a solid blue line with perpendicular blue lines extending inward. Inside this area is a "P" followed by a number. These areas prohibit all flight of aircraft for national security reasons. Naturally, drone flight is also prohibited here. A prohibited area is pictured below.

## RESTRICTED AREAS

Restricted areas are also identified on a sectional by a solid blue line with perpendicular lines extending inward but are charted using the letter "R" followed by a number. These areas are usually because of activity that would be hazardous to an aircraft like artillery firing or guided missile testing or some other hazard to aircraft. You must have permission to fly through a restricted area. A restricted area is pictured below.

# WARNING AREAS

Warning areas are also identified on a sectional by a solid blue line with lines extending inward and charted with the letter "W" followed by a number. These are similar to restricted areas, but with the understanding that the United States does not have sole jurisdiction over the airspace. Many times, these areas will show up along the coast and may encompass both domestic and international waters. A warning zone is pictured below.

# MILITARY OPERATION AREAS (MOA)

MOAs are identified on a sectional by a solid magenta line with perpendicular lines extending inward and charted with the name of the area followed by "MOA." These areas are blocks of airspace where military maneuvers are conducted. You must exercise extreme caution in these areas when military activity is being conducted. Although you are not restricted from flying here, it is wise to avoid an MOA when possible. A military operating area is pictured below.

]

# ALERT AREAS

Alert areas are also identified on a sectional by a solid magenta line with perpendicular lines extending inward and are charted with the letter "A" followed by a number. These areas depict an unusually high volume of pilot training or an unusual type of aerial activity such as parachute jumping, glider towing, or high concentrations of student pilot training. Any flights in these areas should be maintained with extreme caution. An alert area is pictured below.

## CONTROLLED FIRING AREAS (CFAS)

These areas are set up so that people (both public and private) can blow things up. While you should be aware that these areas exist, in the real world these areas aren't on a sectional chart, nor do they show up in NOTAMs (see below). In addition, there's no one to contact. In fact, you will probably never know when you are flying in one, unless you spot the explosion. Instead, these areas are set up so that the activity being conducted stops if/when the user spots an aircraft. Also, just to be clear, this type of area would not include shooting explosives from an aircraft, but are typically just for static rockets tests or disposal of explosives.

## DRONES & NOTICES TO AIRMEN (NOTAMS)

One of the other airspace issues for drone pilots that we will cover here is NOTAMs. Drones and NOTAMs used to go hand in hand. Under the previous rules, drone pilots were required to file NOTAMS before flights. But no more! No matter, you should still understand what a NOTAM is because they provide useful information to commercial drone pilots prior to a flight (not to mention, it is on the test).

These notices provide time-critical aeronautical information that is either temporary or not known in advance to permit publication on aeronautical charts or airport/facility directory. These hazards can be anything from an air show to inoperable lights on tall obstructions or (my personal favorite) a flock of birds going through airspace (called a BIRDTAM).

Your best bet before a flight is to check a flight map like Airmap or Kittyhawk_(they both have apps that work really well too). A recent search before a flight even indicated to me the existence of an emergency, which appeared to be an ambulance or other type of emergency vehicle. While NOTAMS include a lot of things that apply only to manned pilots, like approach procedures at airports or lights that are out on approach, Airmap and Kittyhawk both appear to sift through these to provide only what is important for drone pilots.

The FAA also provides a site called PilotWeb to retrieve NOTAMs but, to be honest, these can be a bit difficult to decipher and doing so is not included on the Part 107 knowledge exam. Prior to Part 107, commercial drone pilots were required to file a NOTAM before flying. This requirement was removed with Part 107 because the FAA felt that it would just clutter the NOTAM system for manned pilots without adding any real level of security.

## TEMPORARY FLIGHT RESTRICTIONS (TFR)

A TFR is issued by a flight data center through a Notice to Airmen (NOTAM) and will always begin with the words "FLIGHT RESTRICTIONS." It will also indicate the location of the restriction, time period, area in statute miles and the altitudes affected.

A TFR can be issued for a multitude of reasons, but is typically in place to:
- Provide safety for the operation of disaster relief aircraft;
- Prevent congestion of aircraft above or around an event that might generate a lot of public interest (i.e., sporting events); or
- Protect the President, Vice President or other public figures.

As a remote pilot, it is your responsibility to know if/when a TFR is in place and avoid those areas.

## MISCELLANEOUS AIRSPACE AREAS

There are a number of miscellaneous airspace areas that are categorized by the FAA. While these tend to be less prevalent and less applicable for our purposes here, they show up in the FAA's guide on what you should study for the test, so we'll talk about them briefly.

## LOCAL AIRPORT ADVISORY (LAA)

This is an advisory service that is provided by flight services facilities for airports that have a part-time tower. The advisory is broadcast on a radio frequency and can include things like weather reporting, airport advisories, or other automated instrument readings.

## MILITARY TRAINING ROUTES (MTR)

Military training routes are exactly what they sound like. Military pilots need to make sure that they stay proficient in tactical flying and these training routes are maintained for that purpose. These are identified as either IR (an indication that they are used with instrument flight rules) or VR (which indicates they are used with visual flight rules. The IR or VR is then followed by a number, which is either 3 or 4 digits long. If there are 3 digits, this means that at least part of the route is above 1,500 feet AGL. If there are 4 digits, this means that none of the route goes higher than 1,500 feet AGL.

To help picture this, this image shows an IFR military training route (in the red circle) called IR720. This means that the training route uses instrument flight rules and has some segments that are above 1,500 feet AGL.

## PARACHUTE JUMP AIRCRAFT OPERATIONS

These are published in the Chart Supplement U.S. and places where parachute jumping is a frequent activity and will include a symbol that looks like the following on the sectional chart.

Just do yourself a favor and stay away from anywhere that you know parachute activity is occurring. This one is common sense.

## PUBLISHED VFR ROUTES

Sometimes when smaller aircraft are looking to fly near busy airspace (think Class B airports) they would prefer to stay far away from larger aircraft, specifically those with jet engines. Published VFR routes, which are also called VFR flyways or VFR corridors, provide specific routes for these planes to fly. They are published on an aviation chart called a VFR terminal area planning charts, or VFR TACs.

## TERMINAL RADAR SERVICE AREAS (TRSA)

A TRSA is an odd type of airspace. Even though it is not controlled, this is an area that has radar and air traffic control services. While communication with air traffic control within this type of airspace is optional for VFR pilots, it is recommended, as it is usually utilized to keep the flow of air traffic coordinated and separated. Again, while not controlled, you can see it depicted in the picture below as a grey box and the numbers in those grey boxed areas indicate the altitudes of the floor and ceiling of those areas, just like they do for Classes B and C.

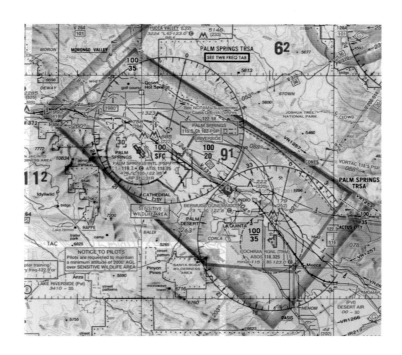

## NATIONAL SECURITY AREAS (NSA)

These areas are just what they sound like: areas on the ground that, for whatever reason, require additional security and safety on the ground. Flying over these areas can be prohibited and, if it is, that prohibition will be communicated in a NOTAM. The FAA requests that pilots voluntarily avoid flying through these areas. You'd be wise as a drone pilot to do the same.

## AIR DEFENSE IDENTIFICATION ZONES (ADIZ)

An Air Defense Identification Zone is over an area where civil aircraft is controlled for the interest of national security. Most notably, there is an ADIZ over Washington, D.C.

## FLIGHT RESTRICTED ZONES (FRZ) IN VICINITY OF CAPITAL AND WHITE HOUSE

As you can imagine, flying in and near Washington D.C. is highly restricted. The FRZ is a 13-15 nautical mile area surrounding the D.C. area, which restricts aircraft movement to very specific flights. It is possible to get a waiver to fly within the Flight Restricted Zone (FRZ) around D.C., but I can imagine it is difficult to obtain. Just don't fly here unless you have a waiver. And even then, do so very carefully and within the confines of your waiver.

## WILDLIFE AREAS/WILDERNESS AREAS/NATIONAL PARKS

Superintendents of the National Parks System have the authority to prohibit the launching, landing or operation of unmanned aircraft under Policy Memorandum 14-05. Because drone use must be done within the line of sight of the remote pilot, this automatically excludes flights in a lot of National Parks, which was probably the idea when the policy was handed down. I guess there have been issues, including one incident where a drone was supposedly landed on Lincoln's head at Mount Rushmore.

Additionally the Aeronautical Information Manual (AIM) states:

Pilots are requested to maintain a minimum altitude of 2,000 feet above the surface of the following: National Parks, Monuments, Seashores, Lakeshores, recreation Areas and Scenic Riverways administered by the National Park Service, National Wildlife Refuges, Big Game Refuges, Game Ranges and Wildlife Ranges administered by the U.S. Fish and Wildlife Service, and Wilderness and Primitive areas administered by the U.S. Forest Service.

While the AIM is simply for guidance and this rule only "requests" that pilots stay above 2,000 feet AGL, you should just stay away from these designated areas altogether.

## TETHERED BALLOONS FOR OBSERVATION AND WEATHER RECORDINGS THAT EXTEND ON CABLE UP TO 60,000

My first thought on seeing this as a topic for the test is that is seems ridiculous that there are balloons on tether cables going up to 60,000 feet. But I guess they exist and presumably for good weather-related reasons. But it didn't take long to confirm my suspicion that a plane had actually run into a balloon tether (thanks Google). To be clear though, the balloon was in a restricted area, and this is typically the case with these balloons for this exact reason. Now, we are officially done with airspace and have sufficiently covered flying drones in other airspace areas. Let's move on to airports.

CHAPTER 2 QUIZ

**Question 1.** (Refer to figure 25, area 2) The floor of Class B airspace at Addison Airport is

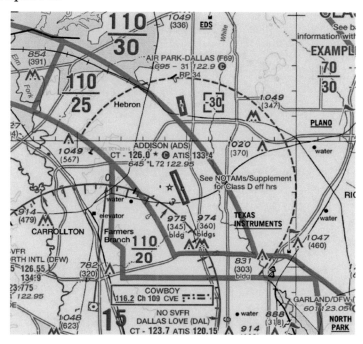

    A.  2,500 feet MSL
    B.  at the surface
    C.  3,000 feet MSL

**Question 2.** (Refer to Figure 22) The floor of the controlled airspace overlying the Sandpoint Airport is

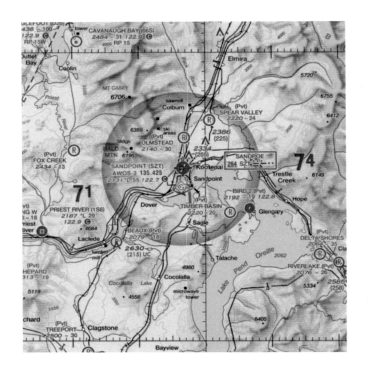

A. 700 feet AGL

B. At the surface

C. 700 feet MSL

**Question 3.** (Refer to figure 23, area 3) What is the floor of the Savannah airport Class C airspace at the shelf area (outer circle)?

A. 1,300 feet AGL
B. 1,300 feet MSL
C. 1,700 feet MSL

**Question 4.** What action should a remote-pilot take when operating in a Military Operations Area (MOA)?

A. Obtain authorization from the controlling agency prior to operating in the MOA
B. Fly only along Military Training Routes (MTRs)
C. Exercise extreme caution when military activity is being conducted

**Question 5. (Refer to figure 25, area 4) The airspace directly overlying Fort Worth Meacham airport is**

A. Class B airspace to 10,000 feet MSL
B. Class C airspace to 5,000 feet MSL
C. Class D airspace to 3,200 feet MSL

**Question 1.**    A

**Question 2.**    A

**Question 3.**    B

**Question 4.**    C

**Question 5.**    C

## AIRPORTS

Understanding the interaction between airports and drone flights is obviously pretty important. This chapter covers what you need to know. Airports typically have two types of traffic flying into or out of an airport: visual and instrument traffic. While instrument traffic relies on the instruments in the airplane and is usually referred to as flying IFR (for instrument flight rules), visual traffic flies based upon visual cues outside the airplane and is usually referred to as flying VFR (visual flight rules). While you will most often not be flying anywhere near an airport, it is important to understand the rules that manned pilot's follow when flying in the national airspace (if for no other reason than to give you an appreciation for the fact that you *are* actually flying in the national airspace).

Another distinction to understand is that aviation in the United States is broken up into two categories: commercial and general aviation. If you're flying on a Southwest jet, you're flying commercial. If you hop on a small Cessna, or even a privately owned jet, this is considered general aviation. Believe it or not, there is a lot of general aviation traffic out there. And while most smaller airports don't have regular commercial traffic, they will almost always have general aviation traffic.

## RUNWAY ORIENTATION

Before we get into the details of a traffic pattern, it is important to understand a little bit about how runways are oriented and when each runway will be used. Runways and their numbering are based upon the degrees of a compass. So, if you look at the compasses below, you can see that North is 360°, South is 180°, West is 270° and East is 90°. Most people instinctively know that North is typically pointing "up" in orientation because that is how maps are usually shown. But if you have a hard time remembering West and East, just remember that it spells "WE" when North is pointed "up." Take a look at the pictures below for reference.

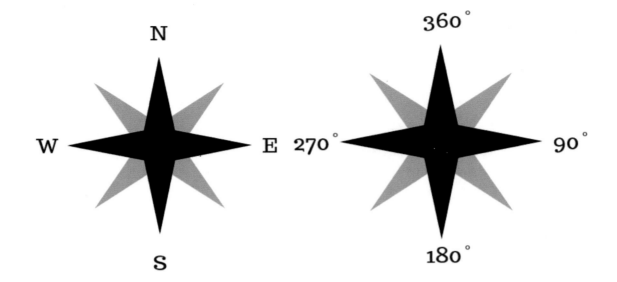

So when you have an airport with runways going both North/South and West/East, you would have four runway numbers that looks like the figure below. What should be obvious in the picture below is that the runway numbers are just the orientation of the runways based on the degrees of a compass with the zeros cut off. North or 360° is 36, South or 180° is 18, West or 270° is 27, East or 90° is 9. Notice though, that the numbering on the ends of the runways are *reverse* of the way they are shown on the compass above. This is because the runway numbers use the compass direction *that a plane is flying*. The compass direction a plane is flying is called a heading.

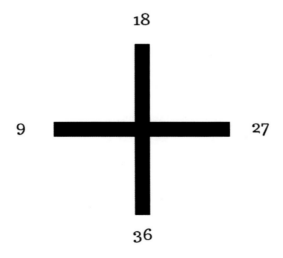

Let's use another picture to better illustrate that. The plane in the picture below is flying a heading of West or 270°, this is why the runway numbers will be "reverse" of those on the compass. We are using the plane's direction of flight on a compass to determine the runway numbers.

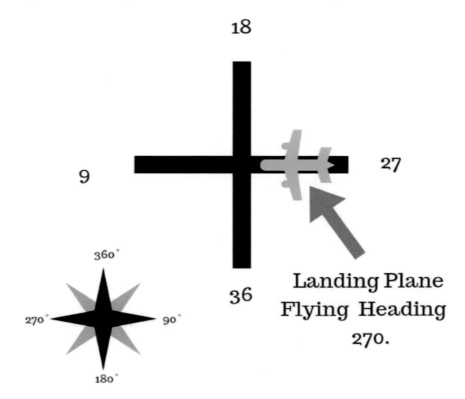

But how do we know when an airport would have planes landing on runway 36 instead of runway 18 or runway 27 instead of runway 9?

It's all based on the wind. When it comes to the way aerodynamics work, planes (and birds for that matter) prefer to fly *into* the wind. So the active runway is usually the one that forces air traffic to fly directly into the wind. I say usually because, as a pilot, I've flown into more than one airport where the "active" runway was not the one oriented into the wind. Pilots will sometimes continue using the runway that is "active," even after the wind changes. If there is no real wind, pilots will ask for the active runway or listen on the radio to see what other pilots in the area are using. The picture below is a simple depiction of the active runway being 18 based upon wind blowing straight North or 360°.

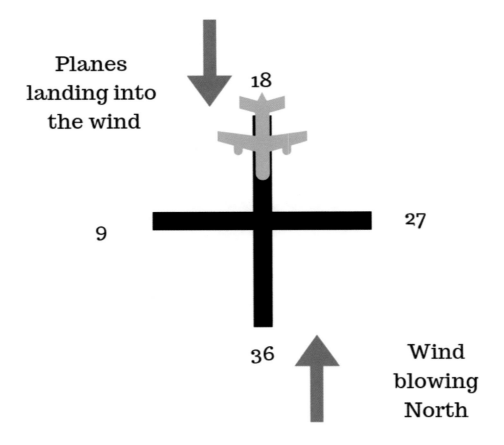

Planes landing into the wind

18

9

27

36

Wind blowing North

I said it above, but it is worth repeating: the active runway should be the one that would force the traffic to fly *into* the wind. This obviously doesn't always end up being *directly* lined up with the orientation of a runway.

What if the wind was blowing Northwest, like the picture below? Here, planes would technically have the option of landing on either runway 36 or 27, since either would be landing as much "into the wind" as the other. In reality, pilots will listen to the reported weather and other traffic (on the radio) at that airport and fall in line with the runway that is already being used. As the picture below shows, if pilots are trying to land on both runways 9 and 18, it could be disastrous!

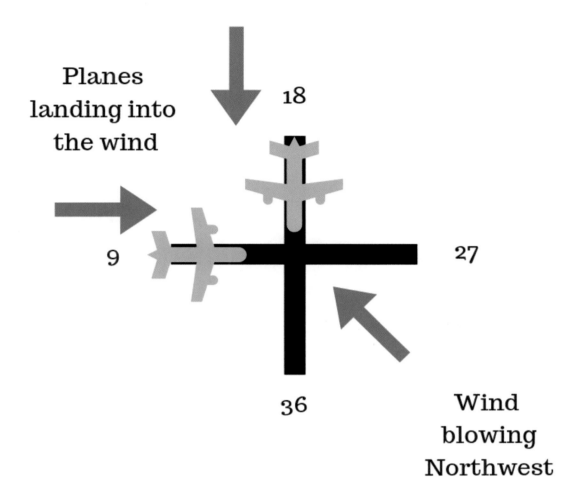

Planes landing into the wind

18

9

27

36

Wind blowing Northwest

If the wind happened to be even just a bit more to the North (closer to 360°) than pictured above, the active runway would likely be runway 18. If the wind happened to be a bit more to the West (closer to 270°), runway 9 would likely be active. You're always looking for the runway *closest* to being directly into the wind.

As an aside, one thing that can come in handy in real drone flying, but not necessarily on the Part 107 test is that planes flying in the pattern getting ready to land will be usually flying at 1,600 feet AGL (above ground level) and descending from there. So if you ever have permission to fly close to an airport or are simply really close to an airport with Class E airspace beginning at 700 feet AGL, you should be aware that you may see traffic at what seems like a low level.

Now that we have a grasp on runway orientation, let's take a look at the pattern an airplane will fly when landing at an airport. Smaller airports that have a lot of general aviation traffic will allow traffic to fly what is called a pattern around the runway when landing. Granted, these smaller airports will also have instrument approaches for the traffic that is able to fly in IFR conditions, but these approaches are beyond our purposes under Part 107 and will not be discussed here. Remember, IFR indicates the use of instruments when pilots cannot necessarily see the ground or are flying in the clouds. Because the Part 107 regulations require good visibility and a line of sight to the drone you're flying, you don't need to understand flying IFR.

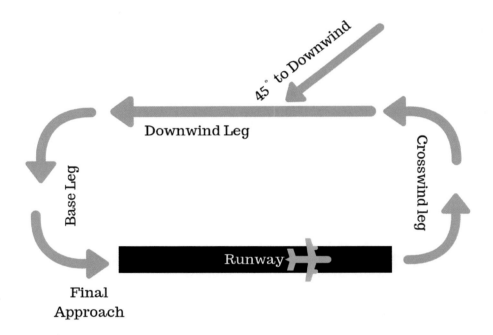

The use of a traffic pattern, however, is very common at smaller airports during VFR (visual flight rules) conditions. Take the picture below for example. Based on what we now know, this runway runs West/East, which means that the ends of the runway are numbered 9/27, respectively. The plane taking off in the picture follows the arrows, taking left-hand turns to stay in the pattern. This is standard for an airport. Some airports have a pattern based on right-handed turns but this would be noted on the sectional and is not typical.

First, the airplane would take the first left-hand turn and fly the crosswind leg of the pattern. Next, it would turn left again and fly the downwind leg of the pattern. It would turn again and fly the base leg of the pattern. Finally, it would turn again and fly its final approach until it landed. At every point along the way, a pilot should be making radio calls to ensure that other traffic in the area is aware of his/her position.

If the plane was flying in from another airport, it would enter the pattern at a 45 degree angle to the downwind leg and enter the pattern from there, as pictured below.

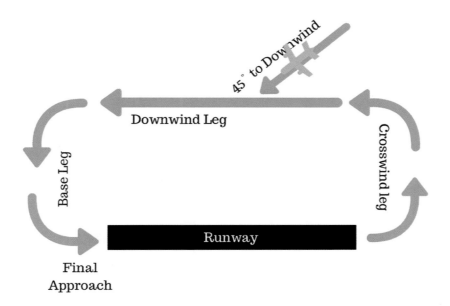

The interplay between airports and drone flights really becomes an issue at larger airports (think Classes B and C), which will usually accommodate both commercial and general aviation traffic. But a small plane flying into a larger airport, even if they are flying VFR, will be forced to follow the same general approach that all other traffic is flying. It makes sense if you think about it. You couldn't exactly have a small Cessna just flying a pattern around the runway on its way in to an airport as big as La Guardia. Otherwise, the larger jets carrying people all over the country would be forced to just wait until the Cessna finished its pattern and landed.

## TYPES OF AIRPORTS

There are two types of airports: 1) Towered and 2) Non-Towered.

- Towered Airports
  - These airports have an operating control tower. These air traffic controllers are responsible for providing the safe, orderly and expeditious flow of air traffic at airports that are busy enough to require this service.
- Non-Towered Airports
  - These airports do not have an operating control tower. Two-way radio communication is not required but it is always good operating practice for pilots to monitor other aircraft on the airport's specified frequency. This frequency is called a CTAF, which stands for Common Traffic Advisory Frequency. We will discuss how to identify this frequency later in this Chapter.

## SOURCES OF AIRPORT INFORMATION

There are numerous places that a remote pilot can get current data for an airport. When flying within the vicinity of an airport, it can be helpful to know where to find this information. Sources include aeronautical charts, chart supplements, NOTAMS, and weather reporting like ATIS, each of which will be discussed below.

## AERONAUTICAL CHARTS

In addition to aeronautical information, which we will discuss below, a sectional chart includes latitude and longitude lines. It is helpful to remember which way these measurements run by remembering that latitude sounds like ladder, which helps you climb. So, latitude runs horizontally like the rungs of a ladder. Longitude runs vertically along the side of the earth.
- For purposes of the test, it will also be important to remember that:
  - Zero degrees longitude is the Prime Meridian. When looking at a sectional chart with longitude lines, the farther West you go from the Prime Meridian, the higher the longitudinal number will be.
  - Zero degrees latitude is the Equator. When looking at a sectional chart, the farther North you go from the Equator, the higher the latitudinal number will be.

There are two types of aeronautical charts that are used by pilots using visual flight rules 1) sectionals; and 2) VFR Terminal Areas. For our purposes here, we are going to focus on correctly reading a sectional chart.

- Sectional Charts - Although we have already reviewed airspace indicators on a sectional chart, there are a number of questions on the test related to accurately reading the various other indicators or symbols on a sectional chart. You will do yourself a huge favor by spending some time familiarizing yourself with the sectional aeronautical chart legend (pictured below).
  - o Antenna Towers - One thing that is important for drone pilots is using s sectional chart to identify any existing antenna towers. When flying below 2,000 AGL, which is virtually always the case with drone flights, it is important to remember that many of these antenna towers have guy wires that extend outwards from the antenna itself and can be very hard to see, even in good weather. Use these indications on the sectional chart to keep you aware of these towers and fly with extra care in those areas.

A sectional chart is a type of aeronautical chart most commonly used by pilots flying under visual flight rules and is one of the best sources of airport information. These charts provide visual cues to a pilot (including things like lakes, towers, highways, etc.) but also provide a huge amount of information about the height of obstacles, navigational aids, radio frequencies, etc. The best place to become familiar with a sectional chart is on vfrmap.com. We will discuss aeronautical charts and how to read them in detail later in the book.

## CHART SUPPLEMENTS

These supplements are available online at https://www.faa.gov/air_traffic/flight_info/aeronav/ and contain information on public airports, heliports, and seaplane bases. These chart supplements provide a deeper look at individual airports and provide a ton of information about them. They provide a detailed picture, list of aeronautical charts with the airport, runways, types of lights used for each runway, navigational aids, radio frequencies, etc. While you should not expect detailed questions on how to read a Chart Supplement (which includes a lot of jargon and abbreviations), know that it has very specific airport information on it.

Aside from just being useful to know that this information exists in the Chart Supplements, it can actually help you in the event that an airport close to where you usually operate has a part-time tower or the airport is only operational between certain hours. If this is the case, sometimes the airspace will change to Class G during the non-operational times and this means you would not be required to get an FAA waiver to fly here commercially during those times.

## NOTICE TO AIRMEN (NOTAMS)

Although NOTAMs were covered in the previous chapter on Airspace, we will discuss them again briefly here. A Notice to Airmen or NOTAM is time critical information that is usually temporary in nature or might not be known enough in advance that it would get published on a chart. There is a national system that distributes NOTAMs, which is available at https://www.notams.faa.gov/. For our purposes, the easiest way to access a NOTAM would be through a system like Airmap or Kittyhawk.

The most recognized type of NOTAM is a temporary flight restriction or TFR. These are most commonly used for stadium or arena events as well as when the President (or someone else important) is flying into or out of an airport.

## AUTOMATED TERMINAL INFORMATION SERVICE (ATIS)

This is recording of local weather conditions and other important non-control information that is broadcast on a local frequency in a looped format. If an airport has this service, it will appear on the sectional chart next to the airport with the correct frequency.

## HOW TO READ A SECTIONAL CHART

***This may be the single most important section in this entire book.*** Although you don't need to know everything, knowing how to read a sectional chart is really important for the Part 107 test and could be more applicable to your actual flying than you might think.

I would estimate that somewhere between 30% and 40% of the questions I answered on my most recent Part 107 renewal included reference to a sectional. There's just no way around it. You really need to know how to read a sectional chart to do well on the Part 107 exam or renewal. Not all of the symbols on the sectional are as important as the others. The most important symbols are going to be those involving obstructions, airports, and symbols that will mean higher levels of manned air traffic. I'll cover those first and get the remaining symbols after that.

The first step in learning how to read a sectional chart is studying the sectional legend, pictured below. We will go through the images in the legend in this chapter but keep in mind that you will get a copy of the sectional legend during your test. Actually, you will get a copy of <u>FAA-CT-8080-2H</u>, which includes a sectional legend. ***Use this legend***. Refer to it on every question that uses a sectional chart even if you are sure of the answer. These are easy points.

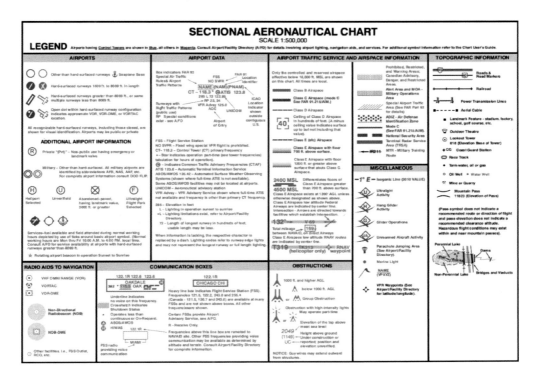

---

## AIRSPACE

While there is an entire chapter on airspace, this chapter will outline the markings on a sectional chart that show the types of airspace and their altitudes because this is a really important part of learning how to read a sectional chart.

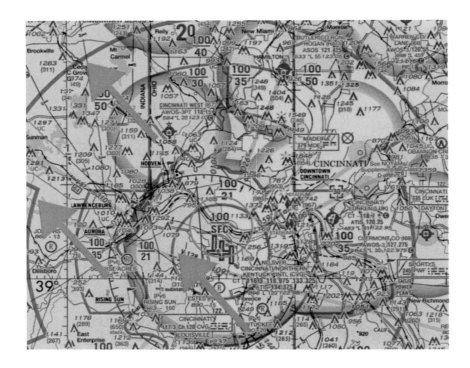

The red arrows in the picture above are pointing to some of the solid blue lines that indicate Class B airspace. And the marking circled above in red is an example of how the ceiling (10,000 feet mean sea level) and the floor (down to the surface) of that airspace.

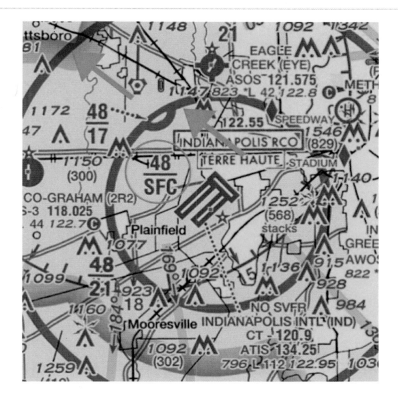

The red arrows in the above picture point to the magenta rings around Indianapolis' international airport, indicating Class C airspace. Again, the area circled in red above indicates the ceiling and the floor of the airspace within that area.

The red arrow in this next picture (above) shows an airport surrounded by Class D airspace. Remember, Class D airspace is indicated by the dashed blue line. Additionally, while Classes B and C have the fraction numbers to indicate the floor and ceiling of the airspace, Class D is a bit different. Class D airspace will begin at the ground and extend upward. The ceiling in Class D airspace is shown by the symbol that is circled above in red, where the number represents the ceiling in hundreds of feet. In this example, the ceiling of the Class D airspace is 3,400 mean sea level (MSL). If you ever see a ceiling symbol with a minus in front of it, this just means that the ceiling is up to *but not including* the number provided.

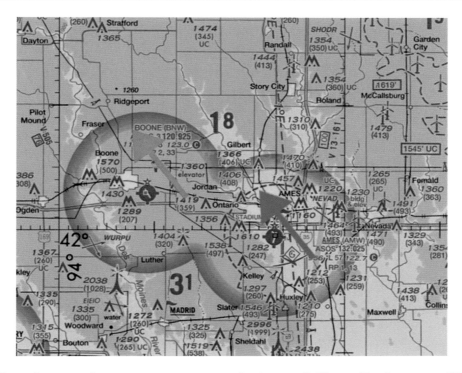

The picture above covers two variations of Class E airspace. First, you need to know that Class E airspace is always going to be measured using above ground level (AGL) as a measurement instead of mean sea level (MSL) on a sectional chart. This is different than other airspace types, which typically use MSL. Above, the red arrow is pointing to the faded magenta ring, which represents Class E airspace beginning at 700 feet AGL. The blue arrow is pointing to the dashed magenta ring, which represents that, inside of the ring, Class E airspace extends down to the ground. There is one other way that Class E airspace will show up on a sectional, and it is called Class E enroute airspace. It is not associated with an airport, but it will be shown on a sectional with a faded blue line. While it is important to understand this for the Part 107 knowledge exam, enroute Class E airspace begins at 1,200 feet AGL and will usually not be an issue when flying a drone. Either way, know that it exists. There are other variations on Class E airspace, but that is covered in more detail in the chapter on airspace. For purposes of how to read a sectional chart, these three variations cover the ways that Class E airspace will show up.

One final thing to note on airspace. The type of hashed line below *does not* indicate any type of airspace.

How to Read a Sectional Chart                                                    53

Instead, it will always have something at the middle to show manned pilots that there is a navigational aid there. Take a look at the variations of navigational aids on the sectional legend if you need to.

Likewise, the light blue lines like the one shown below are called victor airways. These are routes that manned pilots use between navigational aids and *do not* indicate any type of airspace.

## OBSTRUCTIONS & TOPOGRAPHIC INFORMATION

The next type of symbols we will look at are symbols that relate to physical obstructions or points of reference on the ground. As far as obstructions go, there are symbols for objects that are less than 1,000 feet AGL, will have a symbol that looks something like the picture below.

The top number in our example, 1,153, indicates the object's height above mean sea level. The bottom number in parentheses, in our example 305, indicates the height above the ground. The lower number will always be in parentheses. If there is no lower number, or the letters UC show up, this means that the obstruction is under construction or has been reported but its elevation is unverified. There is no easy way to remember this. Just practice. The good news is that the numbers remain the same on the rest of the obstruction symbols.

For obstructions higher than 1,000 feet AGL, the symbol will look like the below image. If the tower has lightning bolts coming out from the top (as pictured below), this just means it has a light.

An obstruction that is less than 1,000 AGL can also be lighted and would look like the image below:

When there are multiple obstructions grouped together, it will look like one of these two pictures:

There are also a number of visual points of reference for manned pilots that you should know. These are all pretty self-explanatory but I'll go over them briefly here.

Double gray lines with a road sign like the picture to the right indicate a larger road or highway.

Single gray lines with a road sign like the picture to the right indicate a smaller road.

These are power lines:

This is a racetrack.

This is an outdoor theater.

This is a rock quarry.

There are other ground landmarks that show up, like oil wells and water tanks, but these are provided in the sectional legend, and we don't need to see all of them here.

**Scan the QR code to check out the video test question on identifying obstructions on a sectional chart**

Water features like lakes and rivers also show up on the sectional chart. In the picture below, the lake is the light blue section, and the river is the snaking blue line.

## MISCELLANEOUS TRAFFIC SYMBOLS

There are a number of symbols that don't really fit into a specific category, other than to say that they indicate some type of air traffic.

The image below indicates regular parachute activity, which is certainly something you'd want to be aware of if you're flying a drone nearby.

The magenta flag to the right indicates a VRF checkpoint, and the black words "BUCKEYE LAKE" provide the name of the checkpoint. These are used by manned pilots as a reference on their way to and from another location, which means that there will be a higher number of VFR pilots flying to/from this location.

Finally, the picture to the right here indicates glider traffic. If the diamond had a "U" in it, the symbol would indicate ultralight activity. If the diamond had an "H" inside it, the symbol would indicate hang glider activity. If the diamond had "UA" inside it, the symbol would indicate unmanned aircraft activity.

Scan the QR code to check out the video test question on how to read a sectional chart.

## AIRPORTS

One thing that holds true for all airport markings: If the airport marking is magenta, it is uncontrolled. If it is blue, it is controlled.

This airport is for public use but has no hard-surfaced runway longer than 1,500 feet.

This airport has one hard-surfaced runway that is between 1,500 feet to 8,069 feet in length.

Notice that this airport is not a circle. Each individual outline represents a runway, but the lack of a circle here indicates that this airport has at least one runway that is longer than 8,069 feet in length.

This airport has a lot going on but I'm only going to address one part of this symbol here. We will look at the others below. This symbol is important because of the open dot within the circle. This dot indicated the location of a navigational aid for pilots (either a VOR, VOR-DME, or VORTAC).

This symbol indicates a private airport. If you open up a sectional, you will see this type of airport all over the place. These are really only good for pilots as a landmark or in the event of an emergency because they aren't open to the public.

This indicates that the airport is military and has a runway that is not hard-surfaced.

This is a helipad. Don't expect any fixed wing aircraft here, but this symbol can be very helpful to make you aware of helicopter traffic in the area. This is way more of a hazard when flying a drone than most fixed wing aircraft.

This indicates that the length of the runway is unverified.

This is an airport that is abandoned. It is just there for its landmark value and to make sure that pilots don't land there.

This indicates an ultralight flight park.

The star on top of this airport indicates that this airport has a rotating beacon that operates from sunset to sunrise. Civilian land airports will have a green and white rotating beacon.

The tick marks coming out of this airport indicate that the airport has fuel service.

This is a sea plane base.

When you see this information on a sectional, it may just look like a jumble of numbers and letters because, sometimes, that's what it is. But, each set of numbers and letters means something, and we're going to review this information here. We will be using this same example for each piece of information.

The red rectangle below shows the name of the airport. Here it is "NEWARK HEATH (VTA)". In the United states, each airport has a three-digit code. The code for Newark Heath airport is "VTA."

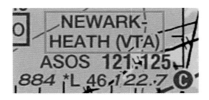

The red rectangle below shows that the airport has an Automated Surface Observing System or ASOS, which can be accessed on frequency 121.125. The next section on radio communications covers this in more depth.

The red rectangle below shows that the airport altitude is 884 feet above mean sea level.

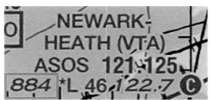

The red rectangle below shows that the airport has lighting, which is the "L," but the asterisk indicates that the lighting has limitations, and you should check an airport facility directory to find out more about the limitation.

The red rectangle below is to show the longest runway in hundreds of feet. So here, "46" indicates that the longest runway is 4,600 feet long. This is helpful for manned pilots because some aircraft require longer runways than others.

The red rectangle below tells you the UNICOM frequency, which is 122.7. The C inside a circle indicates that the UNICOM is also the Common Traffic Advisory Frequency or CTAF. For more information on radio frequencies, check out the next section in this chapter.

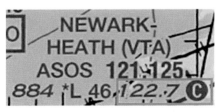

Learning how to read a sectional chart will take some time, mostly because it appears so completely overwhelming at first. But if you study the sectional legend and take your time, you can typically figure out the questions asked on the Part 107 exam.

## RADIO COMMUNICATION

Believe it or not, radio communication still plays a really vital role in safe air travel. But radio communication for drone pilots may seems like too much. This section explains why it isn't.

In most situations, it is one of the only way pilots send and receive communications before, during and after a flight. Although, you may be reading this thinking "it is great that pilots need to use radio communication, but what on earth does this have to do with me piloting a drone"? As I've said before, a lot of it boils down to having an appreciation for flying in the national airspace. But with radio communication, there are actually times when it would be really helpful to a drone pilot to have a basic understanding of the language used on aviation radio calls. In particular, it would be really helpful if/when you are flying close to an airport, large or small, as it will make you much more aware of the amount and location of traffic in the area.

## RADIO FREQUENCIES

There are a number of common radio frequencies used for various purposes. These are provided below with a short explanation of the use for each. No need to memorize every detail, but you should know what frequency you need to tune into in order get certain pieces of information and where they are used in various types of radio communication.

## COMMON TRAFFIC ADVISORY FREQUENCY (CTAF)

CTAF stands for Common Traffic Advisory Frequency. It is a term that is used broadly for a frequency used to coordinate arrivals, departures, positions of aircraft, etc. at an airport. This frequency can come in many different forms depending on the airport. Two of the most common varieties of a CTAF are UNICOM (for Universal Integrated Community) and MULTICOM (which is not an abbreviation or acronym for anything).

A UNICOM frequency is usually used at airports that have a low amount of general aviation traffic and also do not have an active control tower. At some airports, the UNICOM may have a staff member receiving radio communication (in addition to any other pilots) and can provide information like weather, wind, active runways, etc. Sometimes the UNICOM will be operated by a company located at the airport that can provide fuel service or get a taxi for a landing pilot. A UNICOM station will be listed on a sectional chart if the airport has one. Check out the section in this book on reading a sectional to see where that info shows up on a sectional chart.

A MULTICOM frequency in the United States will always be 122.9 MHz. This frequency does *not* have a ground station or anyone at the airport providing information or services. Instead, this frequency is used just for the purpose of allowing air traffic to provide location information to one another.

Some airports have what is called a flight service station or FSS. An FSS is an air traffic facility that provides information and services to pilots but is not air traffic control. Instead, these facilities provide a number of flight related services to pilots. This could include NOTAMs, filing flight plans, submitting pilot reports or getting weather reports. Additionally, if you call 1-800-WX-BRIEF to get a weather briefing, you will be transferred to the weather service for the local FSS. While this all may seem very similar to a UNICOM, just know that an FSS is fully staffed and provides much more comprehensive services than a UNICOM.

## AUTOMATED WEATHER OBSERVING SYSTEMS (AWOS) & AUTOMATED SURFACE OBSERVING SYSTEM (ASOS)

AWOS or an Automated Weather Observing Systems is an automated, configurable weather system at an airport that provides looped, real-time information and reports on weather conditions at an airport.

ASOS or an Automated Surface Observing System is another type of automated weather station, but is more sophisticated than an AWOS and can actually gather enough information to generate weather forecasts. It can tell a pilot the type and intensity of precipitation, visibility issues caused by fog or haze, and track shifts in the wind.

## RADIO COMMUNICATION PROCEDURES

## AVIATION ALPHABET

It may seem that the aviation alphabet is just a way to make people that don't know it feel like they're on the outside of an inside joke. But, in reality, we've all been on the phone, trying to give out our e-mail address when the person on the other end of the phone swears that it started with a "B" instead of a "D". You correct them by saying, "no, D as in dog." And now you understand the need for a phonetic alphabet when the primary communication device you use is a radio.

The aviation alphabet is really just a uniform way to make sure that the people on both ends of the radio communication really understand what was said. The implications of a mis-communication when it comes to air traffic is a lot worse than not getting an e-mail. The below infographic includes all of the proper words and their pronunciations for each letter of the alphabet. I didn't include numbers because with the exception of nine (which is said as "niner"), the numbers are all just said like you normally would say them.

# A DRONE PILOT'S GUIDE TO THE AVIATION ALPHABET

thelegaldrone.com

| LETTER | WORD | PHONETICS |
|---|---|---|
| A | ALFA | AL-FAH |
| B | BRAVO | BRAH-VOH |
| C | CHARLIE | CHAR-LEE |
| D | DELTA | DELL-TAH |
| E | ECHO | ECK-OH |
| F | FOXTROT | FOKS-TROT |
| G | GOLF | GOLF |
| H | HOTEL | HOH-TEL |
| I | INDIA | IN-DEE-AH |
| J | JULIETT | JEW-LEE-ETT |
| K | KILO | KEY-LOH |
| L | LIMA | LEE-MAH |
| M | MIKE | MIKE |
| N | NOVEMBER | NO-VEM-BER |
| O | OSCAR | OSS-CUR |
| P | PAPA | PAH-PAH |
| Q | QUEBEC | KEH-BECK |
| R | ROMEO | ROW-ME-OH |
| S | SIERRA | SEE-AIR-UH |
| T | TANGO | TAN-GO |
| U | UNIFORM | YOU-NI-FORM |
| V | VICTOR | VIK-TOR |
| W | WHISKEY | WIS-KEY |
| X | XRAY | EKS-RAY |
| Y | YANKEE | YAN-KEY |
| Z | ZULU | ZOO-LOO |

MORE AT THELEGALDRONE.COM

Radio Communication

Using the alphabet shown above, pilots will make and receive radio calls for all kinds of information. When dealing with controlled airports, the radio frequencies are broken up to deal with the amount of traffic. Busy airports will usually have ground control stations, a tower control station, a flight service station, approach and departure stations, etc. Each of these stations is responsible for a different part of a pilot's journey on the ground at an airport and into the air. If flying IFR (instrument flight rules), a flight plan is required and based on your location will be passed from radio frequency to radio frequency so that you are in constant contact with someone on the ground. This provides safety and allows for abundant air traffic.

For our purposes, we are going to stick with radio communication procedures that are pretty basic just so that you understand the information that is passed back and forth on a standard radio call. We've talked in another section about traffic patterns. At a smaller airport with a UNICOM or MULTICOM, a pilot should provide position calls on its way into or out of an airport to let pilots know where he/she is currently moving and which direction he/she is headed. When I learned to fly, we used the airport in Murfreesboro, Tennessee. An example of the type of position call I would have made when flying into this airport, it would sound like this:

*Murfreesboro traffic, Diamond One Eight Zero Mike Tango, left downwind for runway 36 to land, Murfreesboro.*

This call starts out with the airport's name "Murfreesboro." The word "traffic" indicates that I'm speaking to other traffic in the area. "Diamond One Eight Zero Mike Tango" indicates that I'm flying a Diamond aircraft with a tail number ending in 180MT. "Left downwind for runway 36 to land" indicates my location in relationship to the airport. I'm currently in the pattern, on the downwind leg for runway 36. "To land" indicates that I'll be landing on that runway. Finally, the call is ended with the name of the airport again for the sake of clarity.

Any time a pilot makes a position report like this, it should follow this same basic sequence. 1) Where you are; 2) who you are; 3) what you are doing; 4) where you are again.

Like I said at the beginning of this article, radio communication for drone pilots may seem like overkill, but even just listening to these radio calls without making any yourself could provide a lot of insight into any manned traffic in your area.

Longitude and latitude for drone pilots can be super confusing because a lot of times drone pilots don't have any experience flying. The most important thing to remember is that latitude sounds like ladder, and the lines of latitude run along the earth like the rungs on a ladder when you climb it (West/East). Longitude is like the two long parts of the ladder that run up and down (North/South). This picture is VERY basic, but is a good visual understanding of lines of latitude (in blue) and lines of longitude (in red).

Each line of latitude and longitude is measures in "degrees." Zero degrees longitude is the Prime Meridian, which runs through Greenwich, England. When looking at a sectional chart with longitude lines, the farther West you go from the Prime Meridian, the higher the longitudinal number will be. Everyone is also familiar with the Equator, which is zero degrees in latitude. When looking at a sectional chart, the farther north you go from the Equator, the higher the latitudinal number will be.

## PUTTING LATITUDE &LONGITUDE INTO PRACTICE

Let's put all of this into practice because it makes a lot more sense when you see it in action. The picture below shows a piece of a sectional map with marks indicating 84°N longitude and 39° W latitude. I've circled these marks in red so that they are easily visible.

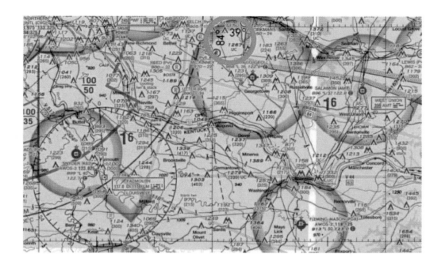

In between each degree line for latitude and longitude, the hash marks are measured in "minutes." Just like the minutes of an hour, there are 60 minutes between each "degree" line. Taking the same picture I used above, I've made the lines of longitude (and the 30 minute lines) red.

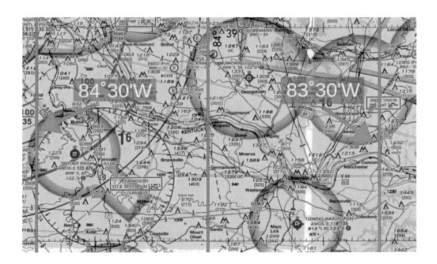

Remember, the farther West you go, the larger the longitudinal numbers will get. So, New York will have a lower longitudinal number than Los Angeles because it is closer to the Prime Meridian.

Again, using the same picture that I used above, the picture below shows each of the line of latitude (and the 30 minute line). Remember, the farther South you go, the lower the numbers will get because they will be getting closer to the Equator, which is zero degrees latitude. So Miami will have a lower latitudinal number than Bangor, Maine because it is closer to the Equator.

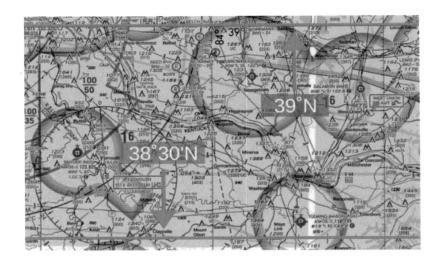

If you're still having a hard time fully understanding this concept, the video below is a test question that I walked through that explains this article in the context of an actual test question. Don't skip this stuff because I can assure you that I've seen these questions on the Part 107 exam and the renewal exam.

**Scan the QR code to check out a really helpful video test question to help you better understand latitude and longitude.**

## ANTENNA TOWERS

Antenna towers pose a specific threat to most drone operations. Most air traffic in the United States (and elsewhere), does not deal with this issue; however, with drone flight, it is very possible that you will be flying close to an antenna tower *on purpose*. For this reason, it is really important to know where to find information about antenna towers (location, height, whether it has guy wires, etc.)

Most of the time, these antenna towers for radio and television will be pretty obvious. What isn't always so obvious, and can be even more dangerous than the antenna tower itself, are the guy wires that attach to the antenna and extend out to the ground. Guy wires are the wires, that extend outward from a tower (sometimes as much as 1,500 feet from the tower itself). I always thought it was called a "guide" wire, but I stand corrected. The FAA clearly calls them "guy wires." We'll go with that.

To add another complication, if you are flying near an antenna with guy wires near dusk, the wires themselves can be almost impossible to see. The FAA recommends staying at least 2,000 feet away from a tower, but, if you are there to inspect it, this may not be possible. So, if you are near antenna towers when flying your drone at dusk, either re-schedule the shoot or be sure you can adequately see the antenna tower and all guy wires. Lastly, just be aware that new antenna towers can pop up and may not yet be included on a sectional.

Use common sense and visually inspect the area where you will be flying before taking off. One thing I've done when on site is locate the guy wires on the antenna and fly vertical passes between the wires, which allows you to completely avoid them. For more information about how to know the height above ground level (and mean sea level) of an obstacle, including antenna towers, see the section on how to read a sectional chart.

**Question 1.** (Refer to Figure 23) What is the height of the lighted obstacle approximately 6 nautical miles southwest of Savannah International?

A. 1,498 feet MSL
B. 1,532 feet AGL
C. 1,548 feet MSL

**Question 2.** With ATC authorization, you are operating your small unmanned aircraft approximately 4 SM southeast of Elizabeth City Regional Airport (ECG). What hazard is indicated to be in that area?

A. Unmarked balloon on a cable up to 3,008 feet MSL
B. Unmarked balloon on a cable up to 3,008 feet AGL
C. High density military operations in the vicinity.

**Question 3.** The elevation of the Chesapeake Regional Airport is

A. 23 feet MSL

B. 55 feet MSL

C. 19 feet MSL

**Question 4.** What is the approximate latitude and longitude of Cooperstown Airport?

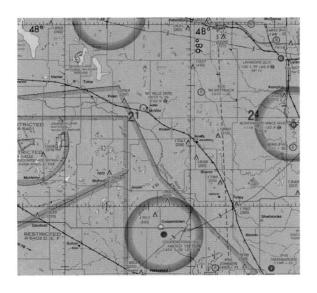

A. 47°25'N - 98°06'W

B. 47°44'N - 100°44'W

C. 48°16'N - 100°44'W

**Question 5.**    Why would the small flag at Lake Drummond in area 2 of the sectional chart be important to a Remote PIC?

A. The flag indicates a GPS check point that can be used by both manned and remote pilots for orientation.

B. The flag indicates a VFR check point for manned aircraft, and a higher volume of air traffic should be expected there.

C. The flag indicates that there will be a large obstruction depicted on the next printing of the chart.

**Question 6.**    (Refer to Figure 21) What airport is located approximately 47 (degrees) 40 (minutes) N latitude and 101 (degrees) 26 (minutes) W longitude?

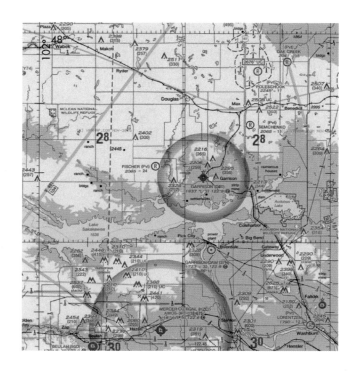

A. Mercer County Regional Airport.

B. Garrison Airport.

C. Semshenko Airport.

**Question 7.**    There is a magenta R in a circle directly to the East of Sundre (Pvt) on the sectional chart below. What does this R represent?

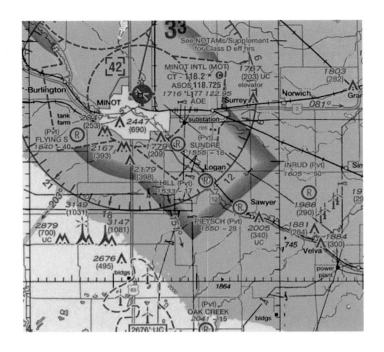

A. A private airport, not open to the public

B. A railroad facility visible from the air

C. A roadway intersection

**Question 8.** What is the height of the lighted obstacle approximately 6 nautical miles southwest of Savannah International?

A. 1,498 feet MSL
B. 1,531 feet MSL
C. 1,548 feet MSL

**Question 9.** The airspace overlying Mc Kinney airport (TKI) is controlled from the surface to

A. 700 feet AGL
B. 2,900 feet MSL
C. 2,500 feet MSL

**Question 10.** What is the ATIS frequency at Cincinnati/Northern Kentucky International airport?

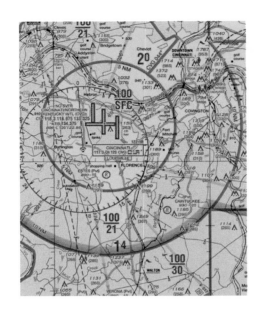

A. 134.375

B. 118.975

C. 133.325

**Question 1.**    **C**
**Question 2.**    **A**
**Question 3.**    **C**
**Question 4.**    **A**
**Question 5.**    **B**
**Question 6.**    **B**
**Question 7.**    **A**
**Question 8.**    **C**
**Question 9.**    **B**
**Question 10.**    **A**

# WEATHER

Just like flying a plane, it is important to understanding some basic characteristics of the atmosphere and the effects of weather on drones. This chapter will focus on some of these concepts, which are important to understand to pass the initial Part 107 exam.

## DENSITY ALTITUDE – WHAT IS IT?

Density altitude is the pressure altitude that has been corrected for the actual temperature of the air. As a basic principle, aircraft performance increases with air density. Conversely, aircraft performance decreases with a decrease in air density. Things that affect air density are altitude, air pressure, temperature, and humidity. I'll briefly discuss each one of these concepts below and its effect on density altitude.

### PRESSURE

Assuming a constant temperature, the air pressure is directly proportional to air density. Because air is a gas, it can expand and contract. This means that when air pressure decreases, air expands and takes up a larger space. Conversely, when air pressure increases, more air occupies a given space. It is as though someone is squeezing air into a smaller space.

To visualize this concept, think of a trash compactor. When the compactor is turned on, it takes the less dense trash and puts pressure on it in order to make it occupy less space. The same concept applies when air pressure increases, it just tends to be harder to visualize because air is invisible.

### TEMPERATURE

When the temperature of a substance is increased, it expands, or its density decreases. Conversely, decreasing the temperature of a substance increases its density.

To visualize this concept, picture yourself blowing up a balloon in your house, where the temperature is a comfortable 70 degrees. You accidentally leave the balloon outside overnight and the temperature gets down to 30 degrees. The following morning, the balloon is seriously deflated because the air inside that balloon has become denser and now occupies less space than when you blew it up at 70 degrees.

## HUMIDITY

There is always some amount of water vapor in the air. Water vapor is lighter than air and thus is lighter than dry air. So the more humid the air, the less dense it is. The less dense, the more it decreases the performance of an aircraft. To visualize this concept, think about the idea that clouds float. A cloud is air with visible water (thus higher relative humidity) and is lighter than the surrounding air (otherwise clouds wouldn't float).

## HIGH DENSITY ALTITUDE VS. LOW DENSITY ALTITUDE

High density altitude is a term that refers to thin air. Low density altitude is a term that refers to dense air. Although these terms may seem counterintuitive, think high altitude=thin air and low altitude=dense air. This is why when you fly on an airplane commercially, the cabin is pressurized. You are flying at such a high altitude, the air would be too thin to breathe, so the airplane pressurizes the cabin and roughly re-creates the air density on the ground.

## PERFORMANCE

Performance refers to the ability of an aircraft to accomplish its given purpose. The factors most affecting aircraft performance are weight, altitude, and changes in configuration that affect excess thrust and power.

For the remote pilot, weight is an important factor to consider. Your drone is made lightweight on purpose. The less weight on the drone, the more excess power the drone has for purposes of climbing and maneuvering. The more weight that is added to the drone (possibly in the form of a camera or other payload) the more you will see a decrease in the excess power the drone has for climbing and maneuvering.

## ATMOSPHERIC PRESSURE

Although understanding atmospheric pressure is important for a remote pilot, most drones have a built in barometric sensor and will measure your "altitude" from the point of takeoff. Keep in mind that although the drone readout will be telling you the "altitude" from your takeoff point, it is probably not giving you an accurate reading of your altitude in mean sea level.

But because the drone provides a rough estimate of its altitude, a remote pilot will likely be less concerned with an actual barometric pressure reading. Despite this, understanding barometric pressure is important because changes and trends in air pressure are indicative of weather activity. Rapidly decreasing air pressure indicates approaching bad weather and possible severe storms.

## EFFECTS OF WEATHER ON DRONES: OBSTRUCTIONS ON WIND

Another unseen hazard for remote pilots are obstructions that affect the flow of wind. This can be anything from ground topography to large buildings, but these obstructions break up the flow of the wind and cause it to gust inconsistently in both direction and speed. This is possibly even more of a concern for remote pilots in that the size and weight of an aircraft plays into the effect of the changing wind. Because drones are considerably smaller than most aircraft, and drones are typically operating in close proximity to the ground, the turbulence created by obstacles could be even more devastating than it usually is for manned aircraft.

## LOW LEVEL WIND SHEAR

Wind shear is a sudden, drastic change in wind speed and/or direction over a small area. Wind shear at low altitudes presents a specific danger because your drone is so close to the ground. A sudden change in altitude at a higher level may be uncomfortable, while a sudden change in altitude at a low level may destroy your drone.

# ATMOSPHERIC STABILITY

Atmospheric stability refers to the atmosphere's ability to resist vertical motion. In an unstable atmosphere, small vertical air movements will become larger, resulting in turbulence and convective (rising air) activity. A combination of moisture and temperature determine the stability of air in the atmosphere. Cool, dry air tends to be more stable. Conversely, warm, moist air tends to be less stable.

**Want to know more about stable air masses? Scan the QR code to check out the video test question.**

To picture this concept, think of a place like Florida in the summer. I have friends that have lived there who tell me that thunderstorms will roll in to Tampa virtually every day. This is because the air in Florida's summer is hot and moist. The hot and moist air creates instability in the atmosphere and fosters the creation of thunderstorms.

# TEMPERATURE/DEW POINT RELATIONSHIP

Relative humidity is the relationship between dew point and temperature. The dew point is the temperature at which the air can hold no more moisture. When the temperature becomes the same as the dew point, the air is saturated with moisture and it begins to condense in the form of precipitation. If the temperature is below freezing, precipitation that is deposited ends up being frost. Frost can pose a risk to a drone because it disrupts the flow of air over the wing or rotor, which increases drag and inhibits the production of lift. The same thing occurs in manned flight, except that many aircraft that are built to fly in weather have built in ways to deal with frost on its wings, drones do not.

# CLOUDS

The most dangerous type of cloud for pilots are cumulonimbus clouds (which are usually associated with thunderstorms), because they are turbulent and pose a serious hazard to flight safety. This is even more true when it comes to the flight of a drone. As you will see below in the section on thunderstorm life cycles below, one of the parts of a thunderstorm is the buildup of the cumulus clouds vertically into cumulonimbus clouds. On the other hand, a cloud type that is usually associated with stable air is a stratiform cloud. Remember this, as I recall this being a test question.

## FRONTS

A front is the part of an air mass that comes in contact with another air mass. The area surrounding these two colliding air masses is the frontal zone. These areas are often associated with quickly changing temperature, humidity, and wind.

## MOUNTAIN FLYING

Because mountains are natural barriers to wind and air movement, it is important to be aware of air movement when flying near mountains. Do your best to gather information on wind speeds and directions before taking flight near a mountain. This could mean getting a weather report or simply paying attention to the clouds in the sky near the mountain.

When clouds appear to be rolling in over a mountain peak, this tends to indicate turbulence on the side of the mountain that is sheltered from the wind because the wind sort of tumbles over the mountain and down the other side. Additionally, where clouds appear to be building into cumulonimbus clouds, this usually indicates turbulence on all sides of the mountain. The point here is simply to be careful and aware when you are planning to fly near a mountain.

## STRUCTURAL ICING

This is one of the things that you need to know for the test, but I'm really not sure how it would ever be a factor in actual drone flight (at least not for the typical drone pilot). That being said, understand that ice on your drone will drastically affect the performance of your drone. Before ice can form on your drone, however, there are two things that must exist: First, your drone must be flying through visible water like rain or cloud droplets. Second, the temperature where the moisture hits your drone would need to be freezing or below. Like I said above, the chances of this actually being an issue for a typical drone pilot are slim but you should know this information for the test.

## THUNDERSTORM LIFE CYCLE

A thunderstorm progresses through three stages: 1) cumulus; 2) mature; and 3) dissipation. Each of these stages is discussed below. This is one of the most obvious effects of weather on drones. I mean, who wants to fly in a storm?

### CUMULUS

Not all cumulus clouds turn into storms, but all storms begin as a cumulus. During this stage, the upward moving air carries the liquid in the clouds above the point where the air is freezing. As the raindrops get heavier, they begin to fall and bring cold air down with them. At this point both the updraft and downdraft exist together and the storm is now "mature."

### MATURE

Precipitation in some form begins to fall, which signals that a downdraft has developed. The downward rushing air spreads out at the surface and is characterized by strong, gusty surface winds, a drop in temperature, and a rise in pressure. Updrafts within the storm continue during this stage as well, creating turbulence and wind shear.

### DISSIPATING

Downdrafts are characteristic of this stage and the rain will stop falling as the storm fully dissipates.
Below is a picture helping visualize the stages of a storm.

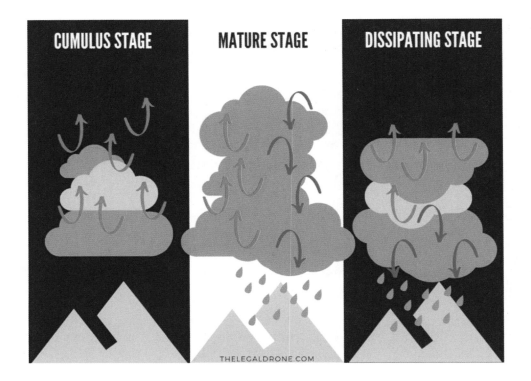

CUMULUS STAGE  MATURE STAGE  DISSIPATING STAGE

THELEGALDRONE.COM

## CEILING

A ceiling of clouds is the lowest layer of clouds that is considered broken (⅝ to ⅞ cloud cover) or overcast (full cover) or vertical visibility into fog or haze. If the cloud cover at a certain point is less than ⅝ of the sky, it is no longer considered a ceiling.

## VISIBILITY

Visibility is the horizontal distance at which prominent objects can be viewed with the naked eye. Essentially, it is how far out you can see big things on the horizon.

When trying to fully understand the effects of weather on drones, it is important to take a big picture view of the topic. Some things, like thunderstorms, have an obvious effect on drones and for that reason, we avoid them like the plague. Other things, like wind obstruction, can be devastating for a drone, but aren't usually very obvious. By taking every part of your drone flight into account before taking off, you are providing yourself the best opportunity to avoid all effects of weather on drones. Visibility is one of those big picture items that you should be aware of.

## AVIATION WEATHER TOOLS

Obviously, the weather is an important factor for safely flying your drone. There are a number of aviation weather tools and it is important that you are familiar with them.

Additionally, it is important to have a basic understanding of the effects of weather on the performance of a drone, as discussed in the previous section.

But as a drone pilot, aviation weather tools can sometimes seem like reading another language. The good news here is that this information only needs to be learned for the initial Part 107 knowledge test, but not the re-test you will be required to take after two years. For more information about what's on the renewal, check out the chapter on getting your Part 107 renewal.

## METARS

The Part 107 knowledge exam focuses on one specific aviation weather tool, a METAR, more than the others. A METAR, which stands for a METeorological Aerodrome Report, provides current and accurate weather depictions that are in a standard format. Below is an example of a METAR with an explanation of each section, breaking the METAR down into its individual parts. Each applicable part of this METAR will be bolded.

**METAR KGGG 161753Z AUTO 14021G26KT 3/4SM +TSRA BR BKN008 OVC012CB 18/17 A2970 RMK PRESFR**

1. Type of report (**METAR**) - There are two types of METARs, which are indicated by the words METAR or SPECI for a special report. A special report is typically issued for quickly changing weather.

2. Station identifier (**KGGG**) - Each airport has a four letter code assigned to it. In the lower 48 of the US, these codes begin with "K." KGGG identifies

the Gregg County Airport in Longview, Texas. "K" is the country designation and GGG is the airport designation.

3. Date and Time of Report (**161753Z**) - The first two digits indicate the date, while the next four digits indicate the time of the METAR in coordinated universal time (UTC). The letter "Z" at the end indicates that the time is given in Zulu. Zulu time is the standard use of time in the aviation industry and is the time at the Zero Meridian (Greenwich Mean Time). Don't be confused by this. The idea is pretty simple. Because air travel requires flying between multiple time zones, the use of one time zone as a standard. The standard used is Zulu.

4. Modifier (**AUTO**) - When a modifier is shown, it will be shown here. AUTO indicates that the report is from an automated source.

5. Wind (**14021G26KT**) - Wind is reported in five digits (**14021**) unless windspeed is greater than 99 knots, when it will be reported in six digits. The first three digits indicate the direction that true wind is blowing from in tens of degrees (**140**). Alternatively, VRB indicates variable winds, which basically means there is no prevailing wind at the time of the report. The next two (or three) digits tell the windspeed (**21**). The above reading also indicates that the wind is gusting at 26 knots (**G26KT**).

6. Visibility (**3/4SM**) - this shows the visibility measured in statute miles (**SM**).

7. Weather (**+TSRA BR**) - First, the existence of a + or - would indicate the intensity of the weather (heavy or light). The remaining letters indicate the existence of some type of weather. Here, **TS** is Thunderstorm, **RA** is rain and **BR** is mist.

8. Sky condition (**BKN008 OVC012CB**) - The sky condition is always reported in the sequence of amount of sky cover, height above the ground, and type of cloud. The height of the cloud bases are reported in three digit numbers in hundreds of feet above ground level. Here, the METAR states that there are broken clouds at 800 feet (**BKN008**), and it is overcast at 1200 feet (**ovc012**) with cumulonimbus clouds (**CB**).

9. Temperature and dew point (**18/17**) - air temperature and dew point are always in degrees Celsius (C). If the temperatures indicated are negative or minus they will be preceded by an "M."

10. Altimeter setting (**A2970**) - an altimeter setting is measured in inches of mercury and is represented by the letter "A" and a four digit number. While this is not necessary information for remote pilots of drones, this is necessary for manned pilots to ensure that their altimeter is reading correctly.

11. Remarks (**RMK PRESFR**) - The remarks section will always start with the code "**RMK**." It can include anything from additional wind data, pressure information or any other weather phenomenon that does not fit elsewhere. Here, the remark section indicates that the altimeter pressure is falling rapidly.

In the METAR we just looked at, the indication in the remarks section that the pressure was falling rapidly would be important to know and understand before taking your drone out because it could indicate the approach of a storm. Finally, keep in mind that all written sources of aviation information use true compass reading and all aviation information you hear uses magnetic compass readings. A good saying to help remember this for the test is: if you read it, it's true. If you hear it, it's magnetic.

Also, if you are looking to get some more practice on METARs, the National Weather Service provides a list of the all the codes used in a METAR at https://www.weather.gov/media/wrh/mesowest/metar_decode_key.pdf. There are also awesome services that let you plug in the METAR codes and it reads them out for you. Google METAR decoder to find one. This is another great way to practice.

**Want to know get a better understanding of how to read TAFs and METARs? Scan the QR code to check out the video test question.**

# TERMINAL AERODROME FORECASTS (TAF)

This report is for a five-statute mile radius around an airport and uses the same descriptors and abbreviations as used in the METAR report. Each TAF is valid for a 24 or 30 hour period of time, and they are updated four times a day. The beauty of a TAF is that although it provides a forecast instead of current conditions, it will use the same codes as a METAR. So if you learn to read a METAR, you will also be learning to read a TAF.

## CONVECTIVE SIGNIFICANT METEOROLOGICAL INFORMATION

SIGMETs are inflight weather advisories associated with large meteorological events that are not thunderstorm related. Convective SIGMETs are issued for severe thunderstorms with winds greater than 50 knots, large hail, or tornadoes. It is called a SIGMET because it is issued to advise of SIGnificant METeorological events. The Aviation Weather Center provides a map of all active SIGMETs and convective SIGMETs at https://aviationweather.gov/sigmet.

---

**Question 1.** What is the valid period for the TAF for KMEM?

KMEM 121720Z 1218/1324 20012KT 5SM HZ BKN030 PROB40 2022 1SM TSRA OVC008CB FM2200 33015G20KT P6SM BKN 015 OVC025 PROB402202 3SM SHRA FM0200 35012KT OVC008 PROB40 0205 2SM-RASN BECMG 0608 02008KT BKN012 BECMG 1310/1312 00000KT 3SM BR SKC TEMPO 1212/1214 1/2SM FG FM131600VRB06KT P6SM SKC=

   **A.** 1700Z to 2000Z
   **B.** 2200Z to 1600Z
   **C.** 1800Z to 2400Z

**Question 2.** Which factor would tend to increase the density altitude at a given airport?

   **A.** A decrease in relative humidity
   **B.** An increase in barometric pressure
   **C.** An increase in ambient temperature

**Question 3.** (Refer to figure 15) In the TAF from KOKC, the clear sky becomes

KOKC 051130Z 051212 14008KT 5SM BR BKN030 TEMPO 1316 1 1/2SM BR FM 1600 16010KT P6SM NSW SKC BECMG 2224 20013G20KT 4SM SHRA OVC020 PROB40 0006 2SM TSRA OVC008CB BECMG 0608 21015KT P6SM NSW SCT040=

A. overcast at 2,000 feet during the forecast period between 2200Z and 2400Z.

B. overcast at 200 feet with the probability of becoming overcast at 400 feet during the forecast period between 2200Z and 2400Z.

C. overcast at 200 feet with a 40% probability of becoming overcast at 600 feet during the forecast period between 2200Z and 2400Z.

**Question 4.** What are characteristics of a moist, unstable air mass?

A. Poor visibility and smooth air.

B. Stratiform clouds and showery precipitation.

C. Cumuliform clouds and showery precipitation.

**Question 5.** (Refer to Figure 15) What is the forecast wind for KMEM from 1600Z until the end of the forecast?

KMEM 121720Z 1218/1324 20012KT 5SM HZ BKN030 PROB40 2022 1SM TSRA OVC008CB FM2200 33015G20KT P6SM BKN 015 OVC025 PROB402202 3SM SHRA FM0200 35012KT OVC008 PROB40 0205 2SM-RASN BECMG 0608 02008KT BKN012 BECMG 1310/1312 00000KT 3SM BR SKC TEMPO 1212/1214 1/2SM FG FM131600VRB06KT P6SM SKC=

A. Variable in direction at 6 knots.

B. Variable in direction at 4 knots.

C. No significant wind.

**Question 6.** At what altitude is the first layer of scattered clouds according to the METAR below for KJFK?

KJFK 041916Z 0419/0524 36005KT P6SM SCT030 SCT 060

A. 6,000 feet AGL

B. 3,000 feet AGL

C. 300 feet MSL

**Question 7.** When would a convective SIGMET be issued?

A. Severe thunderstorms with surface winds greater than 50 knots.
B. When meteorological conditions are rapidly changing.
C. Before any precipitation more than 1 inch.

**Question 8.** (Refer to Figure 12) The wind direction and velocity at KJFK is from

SPECI KJFK 121853Z 18004KT 1/2SM FG 404/2200 OVC005 20/18 A3006

A. 040° true at 18 knots.
B. 180° magnetic at 4 knots.
C. 180° true at 4 knots.

**Question 9.** Which factor would tend to increase the density altitude at a given airport?

A. A decrease in relative humidity
B. An increase in barometric pressure
C. An increase in ambient temperature

**Question 10.** What does the below METAR indicate is the temperature/dewpoint at 200952 Zulu Time?

KCVG 200952Z 20005KT 5SM BR BKN110 18/17 A3004 RMK AO2 SLP163 T0180172

A. 20/18
B. 18/17
C. 19/18

**Question 1.**   C
**Question 2.**   C
**Question 3.**   A
**Question 4.**   C
**Question 5.**   A
**Question 6.**   B
**Question 7.**   A
**Question 8.**   C
**Question 9.**   C
**Question 10.**   B

# EFFECTS OF FORCES ON DRONES: HOW DO DRONES FLY?

In this chapter, I want to answer one question: how do drones fly? Basically, we're going to talk a little bit about the effects of forces on drones.

A drone pilot is responsible for ensuring that the drone is properly loaded prior to takeoff. Each drone likely has manufacturer specifications for proper weight and balance and these should be followed for all flights. It is also important to understand that although you should never exceed the maximum weight, there are other factors that should be considered when flying such as the size of the launch area, surface, slope, surface wind, or obstacles.

Additionally, because drones use rechargeable batteries, there is typically no fuel burn to factor into the weight of the drone during flight. A decrease in weight may, however, exist and need to be accounted for if you are somehow dropping off or delivering something. You should have a basic understanding of the below factors for the test.

## WEIGHT

It's pretty obvious (or should be) that weight has a definite relationship to lift. This relationship is simple but important. Lift is the upward force on the wing (or rotor if a quadcopter drone) and is required to counteract the weight. With a constant weight, the amount of lift will determine whether an aircraft is accelerating upward or moving downward. In the picture below, if the drone weighs 3 pounds, the amount of lift created by the downward force of the propellers would need to be more than enough to lift 3 pounds or else the drone will continue to stay on the ground. Pretty simple.

Scan the QR code to check out the video test question on how a drone's weight affects its ability to fly.

Just so that this concept is clear, let's look at the airplane below. The red arrow represents air traveling underneath the plane's wing, while the blue arrow represents the air traveling over the plane's wing. Do you see how the blue arrow has to travel a longer distance than the red arrow? This is what creates lift. In fact, airplane wings are shaped in such a way to encourage lift, which makes sense. This shape is called an airfoil and the higher the aircraft points the nose, the higher it's angle of attack.

So, on an airplane, the engine pushes the plane forward fast enough that the airfoil shape can create enough lift to allow flight. The concept on a drone (or helicopter) is the same, except that the propellers act as the airfoil and spin to create the necessary lift. A problem comes about though when an aircraft's angle of attack is too steep because then the wings will stop producing enough lift to keep the aircraft flying. This is called a stall.

**Want to know more about an aircraft's angle of attack? Scan the QR code to the right to check out the video test question.**

## STABILITY

This is the ability of an aircraft to correct for conditions that disturb its equilibrium and is typically designed into the aircraft. It affects two areas significantly: 1) Maneuverability; and 2) Controllability.

**Maneuverability** is the quality of an aircraft that allows it to be maneuvered easily and to deal with the stresses imposed by those maneuvers. In more simple terms, this is just the ability of a drone to change directions in flight. Drones are usually pretty maneuverable, especially consumer level drones.

**Controllability** is the capability of an aircraft to respond to a pilot's control as it relates to flight path and altitude. While controllability is related to maneuverability, it deals more with the amount of input required on your controller to make the drone move how you'd like it to move.

## LOAD FACTORS

A load factor is the force applied to a drone to change it from flight in a straight path because doing so produces stress on the drone's structure. The amount of this force is the load factor. For the remote pilot, it is sufficient to understand that each aircraft has operating limitations and should be flown within these guidelines in order to ensure safe flight. Below is the load factor chart that is included in FAA-CT-8080-2H (which is provided during your test). As you can see, as the angle of a turn (the bank of the turn) increases, so do the forces against the drone. In real flight, this would probably be associated with a quick, hard turn and in reality, the load factors on the drone would only be for a moment because the controls are probably set up to avoid high load factors for a long time. The point is, the higher the load factor on the drone is, the more lift your drone needs to create to stay in the air.

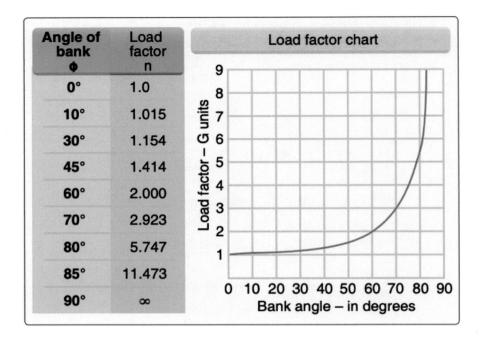

| Angle of bank $\phi$ | Load factor n |
|---|---|
| 0° | 1.0 |
| 10° | 1.015 |
| 30° | 1.154 |
| 45° | 1.414 |
| 60° | 2.000 |
| 70° | 2.923 |
| 80° | 5.747 |
| 85° | 11.473 |
| 90° | ∞ |

As an example, a load factor of three would indicate that an aircraft is able to withstand a total load of three times its weight. Looking at the chart above, when an aircraft makes a level turn at a 60 degree bank, the load factor is two. When the same aircraft makes a level turn at 80 degrees, the load factor is 5.747. Not only is your drone then required to create enough lift to sustain 5.76 times its own weight, continued operation at this unsafe level could cause a system failure. Think of fighter planes and their ability to make hard and fast turns. This is because they are designed to handle huge load factors. Most consumer drones are not.

**Question 1.** A national TV news station works closely with a remote pilot to operate a small UAS to cover breaking news and traffic. This particular remote pilot has had numerous close calls with hazards on the ground and a couple of small UAS accidents. How could they improve their operating safety culture?

    **A.** The TV station should recognize hazardous attitudes and situations and develop standard operating procedures that emphasize safety.

    **B.** The TV station should implement a policy of no more than five crashes/incidents within 6 months.

    **C.** The TV station does not need to make any changes; there are times that an accident is unavoidable.

**Question 2.** When loading cameras or other equipment on an sUAS, mount the items in a manner that

    **A.** Can be easily removed without the use of tools.

    **B.** Is visible to the visual observer or other crewmembers.

    **C.** Does not adversely affect the center of gravity.

**Question 3.** When adapting crew resource management (CRM) concepts to the operation of a small UA, CRM must be integrated into

    **A.** all phases of the operation.

    **B.** the flight portion only.

    **C.** the communications only.

**Question 4.** A stall occurs when the smooth airflow over the unmanned airplane's wing is disrupted, and the lift degenerates rapidly. This is caused when the wing

    **A.** exceeds the maximum speed.

    **B.** exceeds maximum allowable operating weight.

**C.** exceeds its critical angle of attack

**Question 5.** If an unmanned airplane weighs 33 pounds, what approximate weight would the airplane structure be required to support during a 30° banked turn while maintaining altitude?

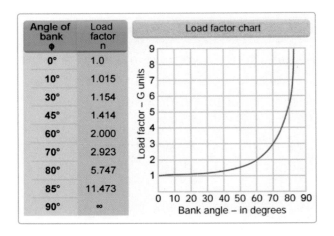

**A.** 47 pounds.

**B.** 38 pounds

**C.** 34 pounds

**Question 6.** When operating an unmanned airplane, the remote pilot should consider that the load factor on the wings may be increased anytime

**A.** the airplane is subjected to maneuvers other than straight and level flight.

**B.** the gross weight is reduced.

**C.** the CG is shifted rearward to the aft CG limit.

**Question 7.** A pilot should be able to overcome the symptoms or avoid future occurrences of hyperventilation by

**A.** slowing the breathing rate, breathing into a bag, or talking aloud.

B. closely monitoring the aircraft's telemetry data.

C. increasing the breathing rate in order to increase lung ventilation.

**Question 8.** What is the antidote for the hazardous attitude of resignation?

    **A.** Not so fast. Think first.

    **B.** I'm not helpless. I can make a difference.

    **C.** Taking chances is foolish.

**Question 9.** You are a remote pilot for a co-op energy service provider. You are to use your UA to inspect power lines in a remote area 15 hours away from your home office. After the drive, fatigue impacts your abilities to complete your assignment on time. Fatigue can be recognized

    **A.** easily by an experienced pilot.

    **B.** as being in an impaired state.

    **C.** by an ability to overcome sleep deprivation.

**Question 1.**   A
**Question 2.**   C
**Question 3.**   A
**Question 4.**   C
**Question 5.**   B
**Question 6.**   A
**Question 7.**   A
**Question 8.**   B
**Question 9.**   B

# DRONE MAINTENANCE & PRE-FLIGHT PROCEDURES

Drone maintenance and pre-flight procedures are not only an important part of getting your commercial drone license, this is one topic that you should be using each time you fly your drone.

But a remote pilot in command (PIC) is always required to perform regular maintenance on their drone as well as a preflight check on their drone to make sure that everything is safe for flight.

## MAINTENANCE

Maintenance on your drones is obviously important and most of the time a drone comes with a maintenance schedule, even if this is loosely defined. It may be in your best interest to come up with a more detailed maintenance schedule if one is not provided by the manufacturer. For the test, the most important thing to understand is that you are required to follow the manufacturer's guidelines for the drone and all of its parts.

There will be questions about this and, in my experience, the answer is always to follow the manufacturer's guidelines. The next best advice is just to use common sense when answering these questions. This part of the guide is not particularly in depth because most of the information I could cover will be too in-depth for the test. The maintenance and inspection questions are pretty basic.

## SCHEDULED MAINTENANCE

Scheduled maintenance should be done at regular intervals and should include everything involved with flying your drone. Below is a list of equipment that should be included in your maintenance schedule, but it might not include everything you need in your maintenance schedule.

- Remote Control
  - Antennas,

- o  Control Sticks
- o  Buttons
- Propellers
- Propeller motors
- Batteries
- Landing gear
- Moving parts (legs of drone etc.)
- Gimbal
- Camera
- Power cords
- Charging stations
- Drone cases
- Firmware updates (for drones, controllers and batteries)
- App updates

Another thing you may want to do is to keep track of your flights, flight hours, etc. This could be great for battery and motor maintenance as well.

## PREFLIGHT INSPECTIONS & UNSCHEDULED MAINTENANCE

First and foremost, have a preflight inspection list and use it. Print it out and keep it with your drone. Sometimes a preflight inspection will turn up an issue with your drone, which can require some unscheduled maintenance. Obviously, if you find that a battery is not holding a charge or has a chip in it, this would need to be fixed before flight, even if that just means using another battery and disposing of the broken battery properly. If a propeller blade is chipped, throw it away and use an extra. Most of this is pretty common sense.

# DECISION MAKING FOR DRONE PILOTS

Decision making for drone pilots is broken up by the FAA into a few different concepts, all of which deal with processes for recognizing hazards and risks and dealing with them quickly and effectively.

## REMOTE PILOT IN COMMAND

I briefly wanted to mention the importance of the term remote pilot in command or remote PIC. The FAA is clear that the remote pilot in command (what the FAA calls the PIC) is in control and takes responsibility for everything that happens before, during, and after a flight.

***If you get a question on the test that deals with ultimate responsibility, chances are the answer will be remote PIC.***

## CREW RESOURCE MANAGEMENT

One tactic recommended by the FAA in decision making for drone pilots is Crew Resource Management (CRM). CRM is all about situational awareness. Despite the fact that your remote pilot's license will allow you to fly without a "crew" in many situations, the concepts discussed in this section will help you think through all aspects of safety in each situation where you are the remote pilot in command. In particular, instead of managing a "crew," in many situations you are simply managing a set of resources (battery life, distance of flight, mental capacity, etc.) and attitudes (being level headed when assessing a flight or obstacle).

## HAZARD & RISK

The FAA highlights a few attitudes that you should avoid and also provides you an "antidote" to those attitudes. They are as follows:
- Anti-authority - "Don't tell me"
  - Instead of having this attitude, you should always maintain to follow the rules because they exist for a reason.

- Impulsivity - "Do it quickly"
    - Instead of having this attitude, you should always think first.
- Invulnerability - "It won't happen to me"
    - Instead of having this attitude, you should always think that it could happen to you.
- Macho - "I can do it"
    - Instead of having this attitude, you should always recognize that taking chances is foolish.
- Resignation - "What's the point?"
    - Instead of having this attitude, you should always recognize that you aren't helpless and your actions do make a difference.

## RISK

For a remote pilot, who will likely be on his or her own, assessing risk is a crucial tool. It is important to recognize your personal limitations and not add weight to intangible factors such as the need to perform your flight. I know clients can be demanding, but flight safety should always be at the forefront of your mind, no matter the weather or the airspace you are being asked to fly in.

## I'M SAFE

In order to mitigate risk, the FAA has an acronym to help a pilot determine their physical and mental readiness for flying. It is IMSAFE

- Illness - Are you sick?
- Medication - Are you taking a medication that could affect your judgment?
- Stress - Are there other psychological pressures from your job or home life that will affect your concentration?
- Alcohol - Have you have anything to drink in the past 8 hours? 24 hours?
- Fatigue - Am I tired or not well rested?
- Emotion - Am I emotionally upset for some reason?

## PAVE CHECKLIST

The PAVE Checklist is another way to mitigate risk. This should be incorporated into your pre-flight planning to ensure that you have covered every aspect of the flight:

- Pilot-in-Command
  - Am I ready for this flight?
- Aircraft
  - Are you flying the right aircraft?
  - Are you familiar with this aircraft?
  - Can this aircraft carry the planned load?
- EnVironment
  - Weather
    - Consider ceiling, visibility, forecast, presence of clouds, icing, current temp.
  - Terrain
  - Airspace
- External Pressures
  - Take an objective look at whether you are able to safely complete the flight or if pride is a factor in your decision. Pride can be a surprisingly powerful force.

## SINGLE PILOT RESOURCE MANAGEMENT

Single Pilot Resource Management is a concept about how to gather information, analyze it, and make informed and timely decisions. No matter the specific process you use, it is important to develop the skill of analyzing each situation in light of your experience level, personal minimums, and current physical and mental readiness.

## PERCEIVE, PROCESS, PERFORM (3P) MODEL

- Perceive the set of circumstances for a flight
- Process by evaluating their impact on flight safety
- Perform by implementing the best course of action

This method is best understood in context of an actual situation. We recently had a job with my drone company where we were taking pictures of a small building for an internet services provider. When we got to the site, we perceived that there was also a cell tower at the location. We processed this information by recognizing that we would need to navigate around the cable attached to the tower and we performed by implementing that plan and navigating more carefully around the cables.

## AUTOMATIC DECISION-MAKING

This concept deals with how someone makes a decision when placed under time constraints, or faced with a task that has a lot of uncertainty. Instead of weighing pros and cons for numerous options, a person will typically try to determine whether the situation is familiar and take the first workable option they can find. Basically, this is the idea that your ability as an expert depends on your ability to recognize patterns inside of complex situations.

## USE OF RESOURCES

As I mentioned above, your use of resources in a flight is key to a successful flight. There are a number of resources in a drone flight to be aware of. These include battery life on your drone, controller, or viewing device, as well as any limitations you have on flight distance or altitude. These also include environmental factors, such a temperature, humidity, noise, vibration, etc. This also includes your own physiological stress such as fatigue, lack of physical fitness, sleep loss, low blood sugar, or illness. Finally, these could also include psychological stress like a death in the family, divorce, demotion at work, etc. Be aware of these factors and do not downplay them when flying your drone commercially.

## SITUATIONAL AWARENESS

This concept deals with the accurate perception and understanding of the factors and conditions within the fundamental risk elements that affect safety before, during, and after the flight. The important thing when you are pilot-in-command of a drone is that you do not fixate on any one factor, but that you have a full understanding of all the factors involved in your flight. In real life, it won't be acceptable that you were fixated upon the wind as a factor in flight and failed to realize that you were also flying close to a helipad with traffic. You must work to keep the entire situation and its various factors in your mind when flying.

The most important thing to remember about emergency procedures is that the FAA allows you, as a remote pilot in command, to deviate from any of the Part 107 regulations in response to an emergency. If you do so, you may be asked by the FAA to report the emergency and the deviation from the rule.

The way I typically envision a scenario like this is that you are flying and, out of nowhere, a helicopter appears over the horizon. You are flying at a legal altitude, not even in controlled airspace, but you are forced to go above 400 feet above ground level in order to make sure the helicopter can properly pass through. There simply is no time to react differently. This is an acceptable emergency procedure given the circumstances. While there are any number of emergency situations that could require you to break a Part 107 regulation, I'm simply providing one example here.

Secondarily, it is important to know that part of being prepared in an emergency is avoiding one altogether. Many issues with your drone can be handled by simply conducting a pre-flight inspection or conducting regular maintenance. In addition to this, if you are using a visual observer or some other crew member, you need to provide a briefing to that party to let them know the plan in the event of an emergency.

There are a number of factors that can affect drone pilot performance. We've touched on some of those factors in other sections briefly. Below is a list of these factors and how they can affect performance. Most of this is common sense. If you get a question on the Part 107 knowledge exam involving the topics in this chapter, do yourself a favor and choose the safest one. Safety is the FAA's main priority and they want you to keep safe flying top of mind.

## HYPERVENTILATION

This is the excessive rate and depth of breathing that leads to an abnormal loss of carbon dioxide, upsetting the balance between oxygen and carbon dioxide. Symptoms include visual impairment, a lightheaded or dizzy sensation, tingling or hot and cold sensations and muscle spasms. Treatment for this condition includes simply slowing the rate of breathing or breathing into a bag.

## STRESS

This is your body's response to physical and psychological demands that are placed upon it. Stress can be caused by a lot of things and typically falls into one of two categories: acute (short term) and chronic (long term). Pilots should be aware of both types of stress in their lives and ensure that their performance as a pilot is not affected.

## FATIGUE

This condition is commonly associated with pilot error and also occurs as acute or chronic fatigue. Acute fatigue can be prevented by proper diet and adequate rest or sleep. A drone pilot should not fly if under the effects of acute fatigue. Those suffering from chronic fatigue should consult a physician.

## DEHYDRATION

This condition is the critical loss of water from the body. Obviously, it is important to stay hydrated, whether you are flying or not. Try carrying a water bottle and staying ahead of your thirst.

## HEATSTROKE

This condition is caused by any inability of the body to control its own temperature. It commonly occurs when dehydrated. Stay hydrated.

## DRUGS

Aside from illegal drug, which should obviously be avoided, there are thousands of legal, over the counter or prescription drugs that have been approved by the FDA. Be wary of those medications that potentially cause adverse side-effects (drowsiness or cognitive deficits).

## ALCOHOL

Obviously, alcohol impairs the efficiency of the human body. It is important to recognize that you should avoid piloting a drone or aircraft of any kind (or cars and machinery for that matter) while intoxicated. These activities should also be avoided if you are hungover, as your body is still under the influence of alcohol. You must avoid flying for at least 8 hours and your blood alcohol level should be .04% or lower.

## VISION & FLIGHT

A remote pilot in command should use a scanning technique that starts at the distance farthest from the aircraft looking either left to right or right to left and working their way in towards the aircraft. Short stops are okay but your scan should be continuously moving about your field of view.

As you can see, there are a number of things that can affect drone pilot performance and the FAA simply wants you to be aware of how these factors can affect a safe flight.

# PART 107 TEST TAKING LOGISTICS & TIPS

Because FAA-CT-8080-2H will be provided to you when you take the test, my advice is to pull up a practice test side by side with FAA-CT-8080-2H. You can use this supplement even when there aren't pictures. Don't forget that it also includes a sectional legend, which can always provide great clues, or help you remember specifics. If you're struggling to remember whether a measurement is in MSL or AGL, maybe the sectional legend could be helpful.

Remember, you will also be provided with the following: pencil, paper and a basic calculator. Use all of these things to your full advantage. Draw out pictures if you need to. If you happen to be sitting for a renewal of your Part 107 drone license, your test will only be 40 questions but you will still need to get 70% (or 28) of the questions correct. Also, your test will not include questions on weather or loading and performance. Check out the chapter on taking your renewal exam. For those taking the test for the first time, you will need to get 42 out of 60 questions correct (70%) for a passing score on the test. Good luck.

## PART 107 TEST TAKING TIPS

### LEARN THE MATERIAL, DON'T MEMORIZE THE QUESTIONS

The first of my four Part 107 test taking tips is that learning the material is actually pretty important. You might think that you have a good grip on the material, but if you've just been taking the same practice test over and over again, chances are you're just memorizing the questions. I've included two full practice exams in this book as well as a number of quiz questions at the end of each chapter. The questions included in this book come with answer keys and almost all of them are based on the actual test figures you will see on the exam. For these practice tests, the beauty of getting your answers when you're done is that you know what you need to go back and study.

Don't hear what I'm not saying. If familiarity with the questions and types of questions you will be asked helps you achieve a passing score on the Part 107 exam, go for it. But make sure you're also learning the material along the way. The whole point of the test is to make sure that people flying in the national airspace understand the rules for doing so.

## STUDY THE TEST SUPPLEMENT

All that to say, I'm not opposed to getting a leg up on the test when you can. You have every reason to study in ways that will help you learn the material as well as in ways that will actually be on the test!

**Did you know that you will be provided with a copy of FAA-CT-8080-2H, which is the test supplement?**

So, let's think about this. When you need to look at a picture, a figure or a legend (including a sectional legend, which I'll talk about next), you're going to use this supplement.

Did you also know that FAA-CT-8080-2H is publicly available and downloadable? Google it, download it and use it to study. Not only will you be familiarizing yourself with the concepts on the test, you will also be familiarizing yourself with specific maps and figures and this should help to spark some more recollection on the test.

Below is a list of the legends and figures from FAA-CT8080-2H that you should be paying attention to.
- Legend 1 – Sectional Aeronautical Chart (Page 1-1)
- Legend 2 – Chart Supplement (Page 1-2).
- Figure 2 – Load Factor Chart (Page 2-2). I've seen this figure on the test both times I've taken it. It is used a lot and helps you to have a better understanding of the impact of forces on drones when they fly. Check out the chapter on the effects of forces on drones for more information.
- Figure 12 – Aviation Routine Weather Reports (METAR). This is another one I've seen on both tests. Know it for easy points on the exam. This goes for Figure 15 as well.
- Figure 15 – Terminal Aerodrome Forecasts (TAF) (Page 2-15).
- Figure 20 – Sectional Chart Excerpt (Page 2-19). The next few are all sectional excerpts. Needless to say, this is heavily tested. Know how to read a sectional. This is so important that I devoted an entire section of this book to it. Also, understand longitude and latitude. Both of these are

covered                    in                    previous                    chapters.

- Figure 21 – Sectional Chart Excerpt (Page 2-20)
- Figure 22 – Sectional Chart Excerpt (Page 2-21)
- Figure 23 – Sectional Chart Excerpt (Page 2-22)
- Figure 24 – Sectional Chart Excerpt (Page 2-23)
- Figure 25 – Sectional Chart Excerpt (Page 2-24)
- Figure 26 – Sectional Chart Excerpt (Page 2-25)
- Figure 69 – Sectional Chart Excerpt (Page 2-66)
- Figure 70 – Sectional Chart Excerpt (Page 2-67)
- Figure 71 – Sectional Chart Excerpt (Page 2-68)
- Figure 74 – Sectional Chart Excerpt (Page 2-71)
- Figure 75 – Sectional Chart Excerpt (Page 2-72)
- Figure 76 – Sectional Chart Excerpt (Page 2-73)
- Figure 77 – Chart Supplement (Page 2-74)
- Figure 78 – Sectional Chart Excerpt (Page 2-75)
- Figure 79 – Chart Supplement (Page 2-76)
- Figure 80 – Sectional Chart Excerpt (Page 2-77)
- Figure 81 – Chart Supplement (Page 2-78)

This list is not necessarily comprehensive. There may be other figures in the test supplement that make their way onto the exam. In line with what I said in my first point, don't use these figures to memorize information. As you can see, there are a bunch of sectional excerpts. Good luck memorizing it all. But if you see a picture of an altimeter (Figure 82), attitude indicator (Figure 7) or glider yaw string (Figure 11), you can safely ignore it for the Part 107 exam.

## KNOW YOUR SECTIONAL LEGEND

This one dovetails nicely with the last point. If there was one Figure I could tell you to know best, it's this one. If you think about it, the sectional legend will literally provide the answer to a lot of the sectional questions you see.

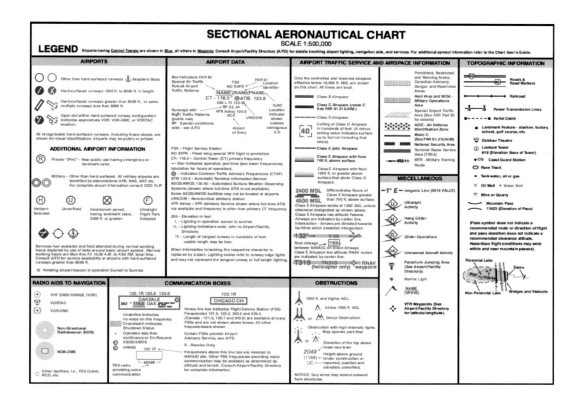

- Don't remember the altitude that Class E airspace begins when the sectional has the faded magenta ring? The sectional tells you (700 ft AGL).
- Trying to remember which radio frequency for an airport is the UNICOM frequency? The sectional legend points it out.
- Can't for the life of you remember what the two numbers at the top of an obstacle are telling you? The sectional legend literally points to the numbers and tells you.

I could continue, but I'm sure you get the point. The sectional legend is a wealth of information, especially once you get to know the basics of the Part 107 material. Learn the sectional legend and start studying it alongside a sectional map (preferably one of the excerpts that will be on the test). You can thank me later.

## LOGIC IS YOUR FRIEND

This tip might seem basic. It might even seem unhelpful. But logic is always my first line of defense in test taking, and the Part 107 knowledge exam is no different. At its most basic level, the FAA's job is to make sure that flying in the national airspace is safe. Logically, the regulations in place are to try and accomplish this goal. I'm not saying they all make sense or even that they're helpful, but that's the idea.

So, if you get a question that asks about the requirements for flying your drone at night and all three answers could be ways to make the national airspace safer, ask yourself which one is the most helpful. Even if you don't use logic as your first line of defense, thinking about answers to questions logically might help you choose between two seemingly good answers. Any advantage helps.

THE PART 107 RENEWAL EXAM

The Part 107 renewal test DOES NOT include sections on weather or loading and performance. Hurray! You can leave behind METARs and cumulonimbus clouds! Because let's be honest, you're going to check the weather on your phone before you schedule a flight anyway in most cases. Most of my clients want video and/or photography and neither of those is particularly great even in cloudy weather, much less rain. Anyway, the breakdown of the recurrent knowledge exam looks like this:

| Area of Operation | Task | Percentage of Items on Test |
|---|---|---|
| I | A. General | 30 – 40% |
| | B. Operating Rules | |
| | C. Remote Pilot Certification with an sUAS rating | |
| | D. Waivers | |
| II | A. Airspace Classification | 30 – 40% |
| | B. Airspace Operational Requirements | |
| V | B. Airport Operations | 20 – 30% |
| | C. Emergency Procedures | |
| | D. Aeronautical Decision-Making | |
| | F. Maintenance and Inspection Procedures | |

## WHAT DO YOU GET FOR THE TEST?

Like I said before, the recurrent exam is only 40 questions, and you still need to have a 70% or above to pass. Sitting for the exam is a lot like the first time around. At my testing location, I was escorted into a room with several computer stations and given instructions on how to use the testing software and the timer was started (90 minutes). You are provided with a calculator, pencil, scrap paper and the FAA-CT-8080-2H supplement for questions that reference an appendix. Keep in mind that this supplement is also used for some of the manned pilot written tests, so there's some stuff in it that you are not required to know as a drone pilot. Don't download this supplement and freak

119

out because you are completely unfamiliar with an altimeter or how to read one

One thing that can be really confusing for a new drone pilot (or a seasoned one) is the whole idea of getting Part 107 waivers or authorizations. Do I need a waiver? Or an authorization? What is the difference between the two? How do I get one? All great questions, which we will discuss in this chapter.

## DIFFERENCE BETWEEN PART 107 AUTHORIZATIONS & WAIVERS

Let's start with Part 107 authorizations first because I think it will also help with the definition of Part 107 waivers. A Part 107 authorization allows you to fly in controlled airspace for a certain period of time.

Part 107 waivers on the other hand, are official documents "issued by the FAA, which authorize certain operations of aircraft outside the limitations of the regulation, but under conditions ensuring an equivalent level of safety." This sounds a little less clear, but basically it means permission from the FAA to waive any of the other Part 107 regulations, aside from airspace.

## GETTING PART 107 AUTHORIZATIONS

Believe it or not, the FAA has taken great strides to make getting an authorization easier. When the authorization process first started out, it literally took months to get any response. Naturally, this was long enough that most of our clients just decided against using drones for the project to begin with if an authorization was required. Now, Part 107 authorizations can be granted in one of two ways. First, you can obtain a Part 107 authorization using the LAANC system. Basically, the FAA has broken down controlled airspace around an airport into a series of grids and within each grid, it has decided the altitude to which someone can request airspace authorization and receive it automatically. To do this, you'll need to download an app like Airmap or Kittyhawk, which will give you the ability to access what the FAA calls the LAANC system. LAANC stands for Low Altitude Authorization and Notification Capability. I'm glad we just call it LAANC.

Like I've said before, I'm a big fan of both Airmap and Kittyhawk but there are numerous providers of this service.

The FAA has rolled out the LAANC system nationwide. Unfortunately, this doesn't mean that you can get an authorization at every airport in the United States using the LAANC system. Far from it. The thing is, not every air traffic control facility has chosen to participate in this system. So, while it is available everywhere, it could be a while before it is adopted everywhere.

If the airport shows up with a green grid, you can get LAANC access, while red means it has not yet been adopted.

While getting into the details of how to use Airmap or Kittyhawk is beyond the scope of this book, scan the QR code below to get to a video about using LAANC with Airmap.

**Scan the QR code to the right to check out a video with more information on how to use the LAANC system with Airmap.**

DRONE REGISTRATION

## WHY IS THE FAA REQUIRING DRONE REGISTRATION?

While many hobbyist drone pilots may think that FAA drone registration is overkill, it is important to understand the current situation from the point of view of the FAA. An entire new industry has cropped up over the past few years and although some people may think of them as toys, these "toys" are flying in the national airspace. Never before has a remote control "toy" had the current ability to effect safe manned flight in the way that drones do now. So the FAA is encouraging the public to think of drones as aircraft, because that's basically what they are. Besides, we've all seen the news stories of drone pilots that didn't get the memo.

- There was the guy that crashed a <u>drone on the White House lawn</u>
- The people that majorly <u>disrupted air travel at Gatwick Airport</u> in London for nearly three days
- The drone that <u>crashed into the stands</u> at a major league baseball game, or
- The guy that was sentenced to community service after crashing his <u>drone into the stands at the U.S. Open</u>.

The important thing to understand is that manned pilots operate under a set of rules making these situations unheard of before drones came on to the scene. And I get it, most people don't operate their drones recklessly, but honestly, there are also a lot of people that just don't understand that what they're doing endangers people. So, although drone registration may seem excessive, it's been around since December of 2015 in some form and it looks like it is here to stay.

## DO I HAVE TO REGISTER MY DRONE?

The only real factor here is whether your drone weighs .55 pounds or more. If you own a drone that weighs .55 pounds or more, it needs to be registered, end of story. There are no other exceptions.

So, a drone like the Holy Stone HS170 Predator Mini or the new DJI Mavic Mini do not need to be registered. In fact, if you go do buy a drone, this weight limit has sort of become the default line between what most people consider a "toy" versus an "aircraft." And this make sense, I'm not sure how much damage you could do with a drone the size of the Holy Stone or the Mavic Mini. Either way, it seems like DJI specifically designed the Mavic Mini to come in under this benchmark because it weighs .548 pounds.

## WHAT ARE THE DRONE REGISTRATION REQUIREMENTS?

The requirements are pretty easy. If you meet the following, you can register your drone online through the FAA's Drone Zone, which is pictured below and costs $5.00.

- The person registering the drone must be 13 years of age or older
- The drone must weigh between .55 pounds and 55 pounds (we will talk about what to do with drones larger than 55 pounds below).

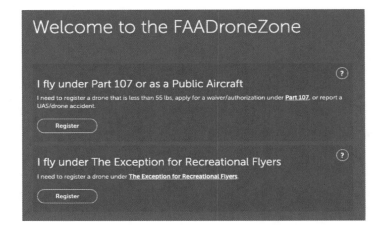

## WHAT IS THE DRONE REGISTRATION PROCESS?

This is where a couple of different paths emerge. Nothing too difficult, but once you get to the Drone Zone, as pictured above, you have two choices. You can either register your drones as a commercial (Part 107) pilot or as a recreational flyer.

One word of warning before getting into the weeds. There are apparently a bunch of websites out there that provide the "service" of helping you register your drone. Don't use these sites. They may charge you more than it actually costs for their "service," but in reality, the registration process is super simple and there's just no need for these services. Also, by just logging on to the FAA's Drone Zone website, you know for sure that your drones are properly registered because there's no middle man.

<hr />

## PART 107 DRONE REGISTRATION

<hr />

If you are a commercial pilot flying under Part 107, you will obviously need to register that way. The difference is that as a commercial drone pilot, you will need to register each drone that you use. When you first login, you will see a "Part 107 Dashboard" that provides you with an inventory of your drones, including their current registration status. As you can see from my dashboard, I have one drone that is currently registered and another that is listed as "canceled." The canceled drone is one that we no longer use and so it was not re-registered on this account.

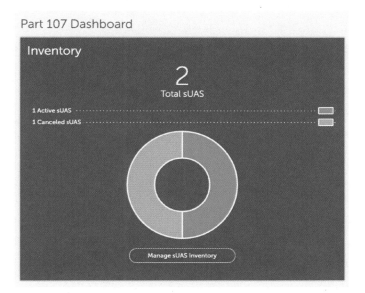

You are also given the ability to "Manage sUAS Inventory." If you click this link, you can add a drone to your account by filling out all of the required information, as pictured below. Pretty simple.

Add New UAS ×

| UAS TYPE | Select UAS type ⇕ | NICKNAME | Enter a Nickname (Required) |
| MANUFACTURER | Enter a Manufacturer (Required) | MODEL | Enter a Model (Required) |
| SERIAL NUMBER | Enter a Serial Number (Required) | ☐ SERIAL NUMBER NOT APPLICABLE | |

Cancel          **Add UAS**

Once you are on this drone inventory page and have a drone registered, you are provided with a list of all your drones, their status (registered, canceled, etc.) as well as the serial number, registration number and the date that your drone registration expires. If you have a home built drone, there is even an option to register it. I'd assume that you would just create your own serial number on home built drones.

Remember, your drone registration is only good for 3 years. What I would do is set a calendar reminder to renew again in three years. The last thing you want to do is forget to renew and keep flying your drone even though the registration is expired.

If you are registering a drone that weighs over 55 pounds, you will unfortunately still have to register via a paper application. I'm assuming a drone over 55 pounds will be used for commercial purposes but I'm also assuming that most people won't have to worry about this. If you do, <u>here's the link</u> if you need it.

## RECREATIONAL DRONE REGISTRATION

I know people generally aren't fans of registration, especially when it comes to hobbyist drone users. Yes, one <u>D.C. hobbyist even sued the FAA</u> (and won) over registration of hobbyist drones. But the rules have changed again, and you are required to register your drones even if you are a hobbyist drone pilot <u>flying under Section 336</u> (check out my article here for info on the other new hobbyist rules.)

What is the Drone Registration Process?                                    126

The difference between registering drones as a commercial drone pilot and a recreational drone pilot is that when you are a recreational drone pilot, you are essentially registering yourself. And the FAA makes this really easy. When I log in to my Drone Zone account as a Part 107 pilot, I'm provided with a screen that allows me to switch over and handle anything I may be doing as a recreational pilot. You can even automatically copy over your account info to your recreational account (if you want) so that you don't have to enter all your info twice. The links to switch between accounts look like the picture below.

FAADroneZone PART 107 DASHBOARD RECREATIONAL FLYER DASHBOARD

Once you've registered yourself as a recreational drone pilot, you will be assigned a number (much like a Part 107 license number) except that this number doubles as your drone registration as well. No need to register multiple drones. In fact, the Drone Zone doesn't even provide a way for you to do that.

## WHAT IF I HAVE MULTIPLE DRONES?

If you have this question, re-read the section above for clarification. Basically, if you are registering a drone as a commercial drone pilot, you have to individually register each drone you use for commercial purposes.

If you are a recreational drone pilot, you only have to register yourself as a recreational drone pilot and then use the number provided on all of your recreational drones.

## DO I ACTUALLY HAVE TO LABEL MY DRONE AFTER I REGISTER IT?

Yes, you do. No matter if you are a recreational drone pilot or a commercial drone pilot. Even though the answer to this question is pretty short and straightforward, I'll expound (like any good attorney).

Remember, if you are a recreational drone pilot, your personal registration number doubles as your drone registration number. If you are a commercial drone pilot, you will have a separate drone registration number for each drone.

There are services out there that provide drone registration labels, which you can just buy. They're pretty cheap and definitely serve the intended purpose. Here's one that's highly rated for recreational drone pilots. Here's another one for commercial drone pilots. They both come with multiple labels as well as a lanyard and ID card. You could also put your commercial drone license in this ID card holder if you wanted to.

Another thing I thought was really cool about these labels was that they included two other stickers, one to put your phone number on and the other encouraging anyone that finds your drone (in the event of a crash or flyaway) to contact you by going to reclaimdrone.com.

What we did for my drone services company was just buy a label marker, like this one. And even if you opt to go this route, you could still use the label maker to encourage anyone that finds your drone to go to reclaimdrone.com. It's a free service. All you have to do is add your drone (or drones) to their database.

## HOW MUCH DOES IT COST?

Again, this one depends on whether you're registering as a commercial or recreational drone pilot. If you're registering drones as a commercial drone pilot, it will cost you $5.00 for each drone.

If you are registering as a recreational drone pilot, you register yourself once and use this registration number on all of your drones. This also costs $5.00 (no matter how many drones you have).
Both registrations last for three years.

## WHAT HAPPENS IF I DON'T REGISTER MY DRONE?

Failure to register your drones (or yourself as a recreational drone pilot) could lead to FAA fines of up to $27,500 for civil penalties and/or up to $250,000 for criminal penalties. While the chances of this are unlikely, it's totally worth it to spend $5.00 now to avoid some legal headaches and monetary fines later. Just do yourself a favor and register your drones.

This section provides two full-length (60 question) practice tests with answer keys at the end. In an effort to best aid your studying, I've pulled the content of these test questions directly from the FAA's study guide and the test supplement that you will receive when you take the test. Although the test questions in these practice tests are not necessarily the ones you will actually see on the test, they will pull from the same information and sectional maps you will see on test day and this should help provide some familiarity.

## PRACTICE TEST # 1

**Question 1.** According to 14 CFR part 107, an sUAS is an unmanned aircraft system weighing
  A. 55 lbs or less.
  B. 55 kg or less.
  C. Less than 55 lbs.

**Question 2.** Which technique should a pilot use to scan for traffic?

  A. Systematically focus on different segments of the sky for short intervals.
  B. Concentrate on relative movement detected in the peripheral vision area.
  C. Continuous sweeping of the windshield from right to left.

**Question 3.** A person whose sole task is watching the sUAS to report hazards to the rest of the crew is called

  A. Visual observer
  B. Person manipulating the controls
  C. Remote-PIC

**Question 4.** During your preflight inspection, you discover a small nick in the casing of your sUAS battery. What action should you take?

  A. Use it as long as it will still hold a charge.
  B. Throw it away with your household trash.

C. Follow the manufacturer's guidance.

**Question 5.** According to 14 CFR part 107, what is required to operate a small UA within 30 minutes after official sunset?

    **A.** Use of a transponder.
    **B.** Use of anti-collision lights.
    **C.** Must be operated in a rural area.

**Question 6.** (Refer to Figure 20.) Who would a Remote Pilot in Command contact to "CHECK NOTAMS" as it is noted in the CAUTION box regarding the unmarked balloon?

    **A.** FAA district office
    **B.** NTSB office
    **C.** Flight Service

**Question 7.** (Refer to figure 15) In the TAF from KOKC, the clear sky becomes

KOKC 051130Z 051212 14008KT 5SM BR BKN030 TEMPO 1316 1 1/2SM BR FM 1600 16010KT P6SM NSW SKC BECMG 2224 20013G20KT 4SM SHRA OVC020 PROB40 0006 2SM TSRA OVC008CB BECMG 0608 21015KT P6SM NSW SCT040=

A. overcast at 200 feet with a 40% probability of becoming overcast at 600 feet during the forecast period between 2200Z and 2400Z.

B. overcast at 2,000 feet during the forecast period between 2200Z and 2400Z.

C. overcast at 200 feet with the probability of becoming overcast at 400 feet during the forecast period between 2200Z and 2400Z.

**Question 8.** When loading cameras or other equipment on an sUAS, mount the items in a manner that

A. Can be easily removed without the use of tools.

B. Does not adversely affect the center of gravity.

C. Is visible to the visual observer or other crewmembers.

**Question 9.** (Refer to Figure 20.) Why would the small flag at Lake Drummond in area 2 of the sectional chart be important to a Remote PIC?

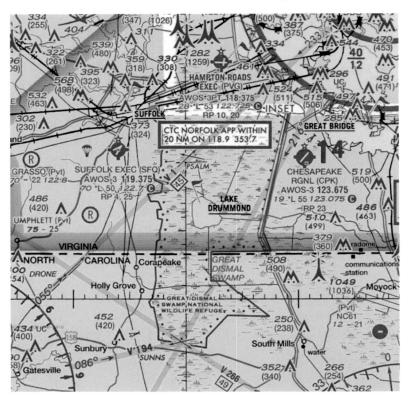

**A.** The flag indicates a GPS check point that can be used by both manned and remote pilots for orientation.

**B.** The flag indicates a VFR checkpoint for manned aircraft, and a higher volume of air traffic should be expected there.

**C.** The flag indicates that there will be a large obstruction depicted on the next printing of the chart.

**Question 10.**     What is a characteristic of stable air?

**A.** Stratiform clouds
**B.** Unlimited visibility
**C.** Cumulus clouds

**Question 11.**     Are you required to use a visual observer if you are wearing first person viewer (FPV) goggles?

**A.** No
**B.** Yes
**C.** Only if you are in controlled airspace

**Question 12.**     A pilot should be able to overcome the symptoms or avoid future occurrences of hyperventilation by

**A.** slowing the breathing rate, breathing into a bag, or talking aloud.
**B.** increasing the breathing rate in order to increase lung ventilation.
**C.** closely monitoring the aircraft's telemetry data.

**Question 13.**     When adapting crew resource management (CRM) concepts to the operation of a small UA, CRM must be integrated into

**A.** all phases of the operation.
**B.** the communications only.
**C.** the flight portion only.

**Question 14.**     What action should a remote-pilot take when operating in a Military Operations Area (MOA)?

**A.** Fly only along Military Training Routes (MTRs)

**B.** Exercise extreme caution when military activity is being conducted

**C.** Obtain authorization from the controlling agency prior to operating in the MOA

**Question 15.** (Refer to Figure 21.) What airport is located approximately 47 (degrees) 40 (minutes) N latitude and 101 (degrees) 26 (minutes) W longitude?

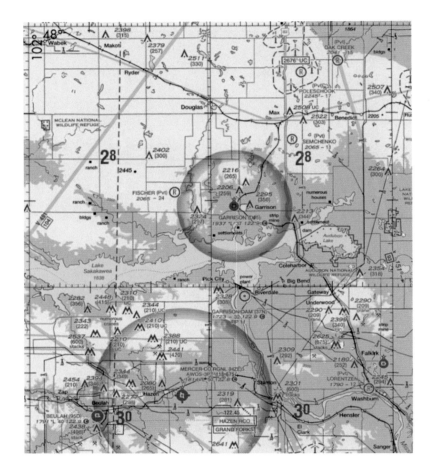

**A.** Garrison Airport.

**B.** Mercer County Regional Airport.

**C.** Semshenko Airport.

**Question 16.** (Refer to Figure 2.) If an unmanned airplane weighs 33 pounds, what approximate weight would the airplane structure be required to support during a 30° banked turn while maintaining altitude?

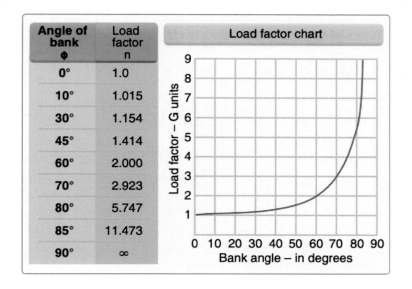

A. 47 pounds.
B. 38 pounds.
C. 34 pounds.

**Question 17.** (Refer to figure 15) What is the forecast wind for KMEM from 1600Z until the end of the forecast?

KOKC 051130Z 051212 14008KT 5SM BR BKN030 TEMPO 1316 1 1/2SM BR FM 1600 16010KT P6SM NSW SKC BECMG 2224 20013G20KT 4SM SHRA OVC020 PROB40 0006 2SM TSRA OVC008CB BECMG 0608 21015KT P6SM NSW SCT040=

A. Variable in direction at 6 knots.
B. No significant wind.
C. Variable in direction at 4 knots.

**Question 18.** The FAA may approve your application for a waiver of provisions in part 107 only when it has been determined that the proposed operation

A. Can be safely conducted under the terms of that certificate of waiver
B. Involves public aircraft or air carrier operations

C. Will be conducted outside the United-States

**Question 19.** What are characteristics of a moist, unstable air mass?

A. Cumuliform clouds and showery precipitation.
B. Poor visibility and smooth air.
C. Stratiform clouds and showery precipitation.

**Question 20.** A stall occurs when the smooth airflow over the unmanned airplane's wing is disrupted, and the lift degenerates rapidly. This is caused when the wing

A. exceeds its critical angle of attack.
B. exceeds maximum allowable operating weight.
C. exceeds the maximum speed.

**Question 21.** The most comprehensive information on a given airport is provided by
A. Terminal Area Chart (TAC)
B. Notices to Airmen (NOTAMs)
C. The Chart Supplements U.S. (formerly Airport/Facility Directory)

**Question 22.** (Refer to Figure 26, area 2.) What is the approximate latitude and longitude of Cooperstown Airport?

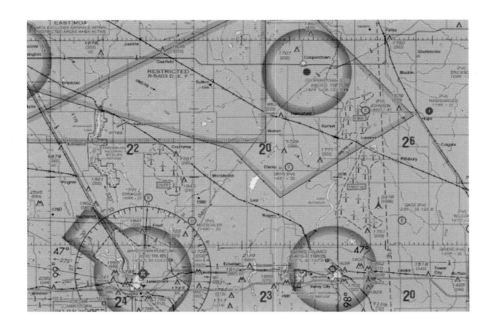

A. 47°55'N - 98°06'W

B. 47°25'N - 99°54'W

C. 47°25'N - 98°06'W

**Question 23.**        (Refer to Figure 20, Area 3.) With ATC authorization, you are operating your small unmanned aircraft approximately 4 SM southeast of Elizabeth City Regional Airport (ECG). What hazard is indicated to be in that area?

A. Unmarked balloon on a cable

B. Heavy parachute activity in the area

C. High density military operations in the vicinity.

**Question 24.**        Who holds the responsibility to ensure all crew members who are participating in the operation are not impaired by drugs or alcohol?

A. The Contractor

B. The Remote Pilot in Command (Remote PIC)

**C.** The Site Supervisor

**Question 25.** (Refer to figure 21, area 1.) Determine the approximate latitude and longitude of Minot Intl Airport.

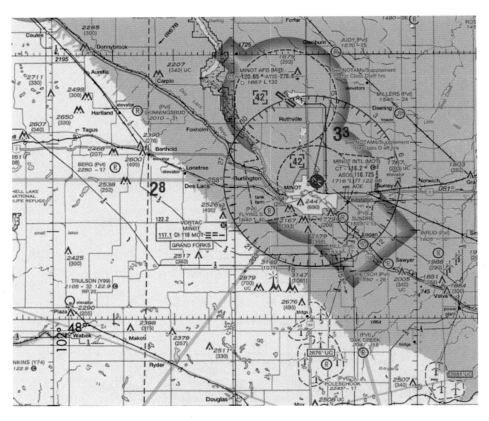

**A.** 48°16'N - 100°44'W

**B.** 48°16'N - 101°16'W

**C.** 47°44'N - 100°44'W

**Question 26.** (See Figure 15) Between 1000Z and 1200Z the visibility at KMEM is forecast to be?

```
TAF

KMEM 121720Z 1218/1324 20012KT 5SM HZ BKN030 PROB40 1220/1222 1SM TSRA OVC008CB
     FM122200 33015G20KT P6SM BKN015 OVC025 PROB40 1220/1222 3SM SHRA
     FM120200 35012KT OVC008 PROB40 1202/1205 2SM-RASN BECMG 1306/1308 02008KT BKN012
     BECMG 1310/1312 00000KT 3SM BR SKC TEMPO 1212/1214 1/2SM FG
     FM131600 VRB06KT P6SM SKC=

KOKC 051130Z 0512/0618 14008KT 5SM BR BKN030 TEMPO 0513/0516 1 1/2SM BR
     FM051600 18010KT P6SM SKC BECMG 0522/0524 20013G20KT 4SM SHRA OVC020
     PROB40 0600/0606 2SM TSRA OVC008CB BECMG 0606/0608 21015KT P6SM SCT040=
```

A. 1/2 SM

B. 3 SM

C. 1 SM

**Question 27.** (Refer to Figure 26, Area 4.) You have been hired to inspect the tower under construction at 46.9N and 98.6W, near Jamestown Regional (JMS). What must you receive prior to flying your unmanned aircraft in this area?

A. Authorization from ATC.

B. Authorization from the military.

C. Authorization from the National Park Service.

**Question 28.** What is the antidote when a pilot has a hazardous attitude, such as Anti-authority?

A. Rules do not apply to this situation

**B.** I know what I am doing

**C.** Follow the rules

**Question 29.** What is the antidote when a pilot has a hazardous attitude, such as Resignation?

**A.** I am not helpless

**B.** What is the use

**C.** Someone else is responsible

**Question 30.** (Refer to figure 22, area 3.) The elevation of the Shoshone County Airport is

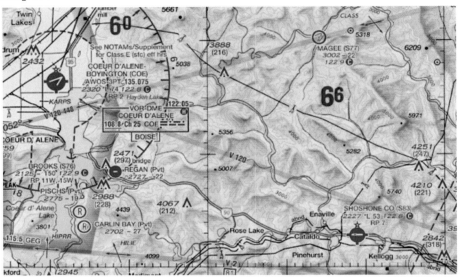

**A.** 5500 feet

**B.** 55 feet

**C.** 2227 feet

**Question 31.** (Refer to Figure 20.) How would a remote PIC "CHECK NOTAMS" as noted in the CAUTION box regarding the unmarked balloon?

A. By obtaining a briefing via an online source such as 1800WXBrief.com.

B. By utilizing the B4UFLY mobile application.

C. By contacting the FAA district office.

**Question 32.** If an unstable air mass is forced upward, what type clouds can be expected?

A. Clouds with considerable vertical development and associated turbulence.

B. Stratus clouds with considerable associated turbulence.

C. Stratus clouds with little vertical development.

**Question 33.** Damaged lithium batteries can cause

A. Increased endurance

B. An inflight fire

C. A change in aircraft center of gravity

**Question 34.** Before each flight, the Remote PIC must ensure that
    A. ATC has granted clearance
    B. The site supervisor has approved the flight
    C. Objects carried on the sUAS are secure

**Question 35.** (Refer to figure 2.) If an airplane weighs 23 pounds, what approximate weight would the airplane structure be required to support during a 60° banked turn while maintaining altitude?

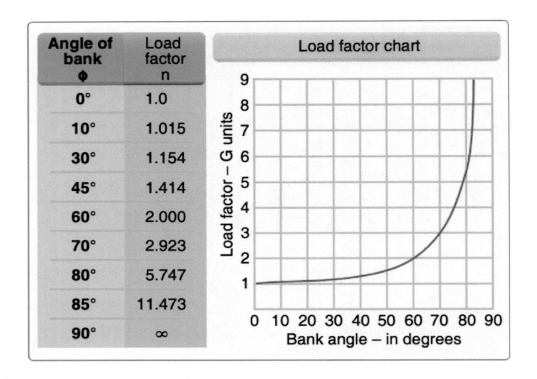

    A. 46 pounds
    B. 34 pounds
    C. 23 pounds

**Question 36.** (Refer to Figure 20, area 2) The elevation of the Chesapeake Regional Airport is

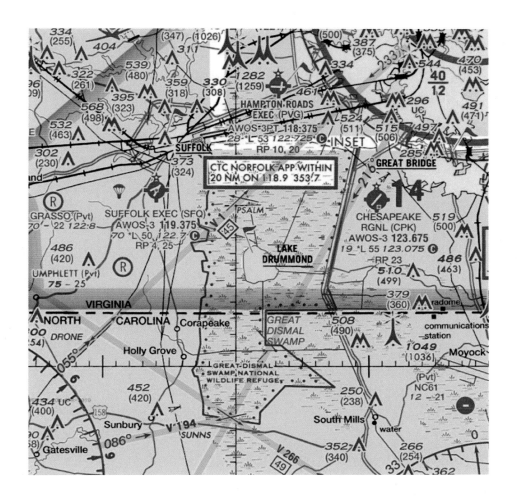

    A. 23 feet

    B. 19 feet

    C. 55 feet

**Question 37.**      Within how many days must an sUAS accident be reported to the FAA?

    A. 30 days

    B. 90 days

    C. 10 days

**Question 38.**      You may operate an sUAS from a moving vehicle when no property is carried for compensation or hire

    A. Over a sparsely populated area

    B. Over suburban areas

    C. Over a parade or other social events

**Question 39.** As a remote-pilot operating near an airport, you should expect arriving aircraft to join the traffic pattern
   A. 45 degrees to base
   B. overflying the runway and turning downwind
   C. 45 degrees to downwind


**Question 40.** To avoid a possible collision with a manned airplane, you estimate that your small UA climbed to an altitude greater than 600 feet AGL. To whom must you report the deviation?
   A. Air Traffic Control.
   B. The FAA, upon request.
   C. The National Transportation Safety Board.


**Question 41.** When operating an unmanned airplane, the remote pilot should consider that the load factor on the wings may be increased any time
   A. the CG is shifted rearward to the aft CG limit.
   B. the gross weight is reduced.
   C. the airplane is subjected to maneuvers other than straight-and-level flight.


**Question 42.** Which is true regarding the presence of alcohol within the human body?
   A. A small amount of alcohol increases vision acuity.
   B. Judgment and decision-making abilities can be adversely affected by even small amounts of alcohol.
   C. Consuming an equal amount of water will increase the destruction of alcohol and alleviate a hangover.


**Question 43.** To ensure that the unmanned aircraft center of gravity (CG) limits are not exceeded, follow the aircraft loading instructions specified in the
   A. Pilot's Operating Handbook or UAS Flight Manual.
   B. Aeronautical Information Manual (AIM).
   C. Aircraft Weight and Balance Handbook.


**Question 44.** When using a small UA in a commercial operation, who is responsible for briefing the participants about emergency procedures?
   A. The FAA inspector-in-charge.

**B.** The remote PIC.

**C.** The lead visual observer.

**Question 45.** (Refer to Figure 23, Area 3.) What is the floor of the Savannah Class C airspace at the shelf area (outer circle)?

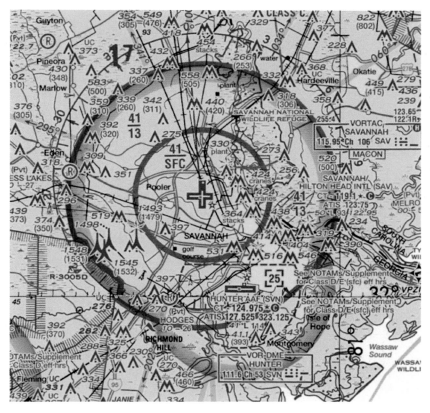

**A.** 1,300 feet AGL.

**B.** 1,700 feet MSL.

**C.** 1,300 feet MSL.

**Question 46.** (Refer to Figure 21.) You have been hired by a farmer to use your small UA to inspect his crops. The area that you are to survey is in the Devil's Lake West MOA, east of area 2. How would you find out if the MOA is active?

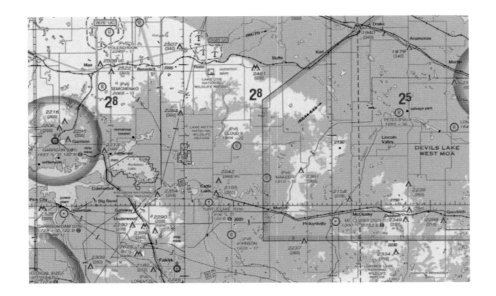

   **A.** Refer to the Military Operations Directory.

   **B.** Refer to the chart legend.

   **C.** This information is available in the Small UAS database.

**Question 47.** According to 14 CFR part 107 the remote pilot in command (PIC) of a small unmanned aircraft planning to operate within Class C airspace

   **A.** is required to receive ATC authorization.

   **B.** must use a visual observer.

   **C.** is required to file a flight plan.

**Question 48.** (Refer to Figure 59, Area 2.) The chart shows a gray line with "VR1667, VR1617, VR1638, and VR1668." Could this area present a hazard to the operations of a small UA?

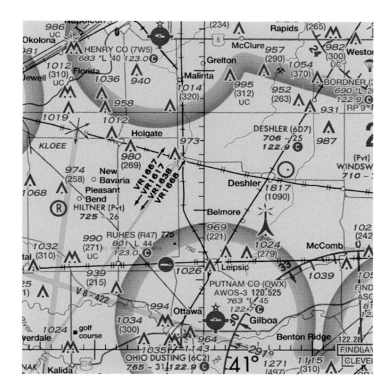

A. Yes, the defined route provides traffic separation to manned aircraft.

B. Yes, this is a Military Training Route from the surface to 1,500 feet AGL.

C. No, all operations will be above 400 feet.

**Question 49.** (Refer to FAA-CT-8080-2H, Figure 26.) What does the line of latitude at area 4 measure?

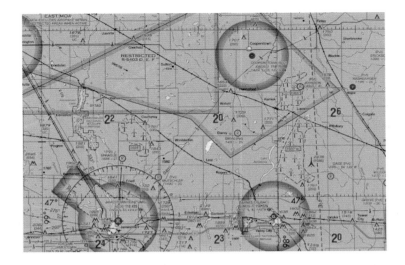

A. The degrees of latitude east and west of the line that passes through Greenwich, England.

B. The degrees of latitude east and west of the Prime Meridian.

C. The degrees of latitude north and south of the equator.

**Question 50.** (Refer to Figure 26, Area 2.) While monitoring the Cooperstown CTAF you hear an aircraft announce that they are midfield left downwind to RWY 13. Where would the aircraft be relative to the runway?

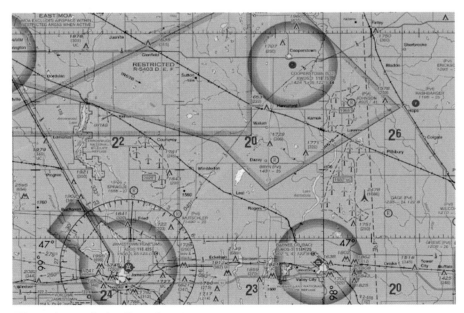

A. The aircraft is South.

B. The aircraft is West.

C. The aircraft is East.

**Question 51.**      You have been hired as a remote pilot by a local TV news station to film breaking news with a small UA. You expressed a safety concern and the station manager has instructed you to "fly first, ask questions later." What type of hazardous attitude does this attitude represent?

A. Invulnerability.
B. Impulsivity.
C. Machismo.

**Question 52.**      Under what condition should the operator of a small UA establish scheduled maintenance protocol?

A. UAS does not need a required maintenance schedule.
B. When the manufacturer does not provide a maintenance schedule.
C. When the FAA requires you to, following an accident.

**Question 53.**      Identify the hazardous attitude or characteristic a remote pilot displays while taking risks in order to impress others?

A. Invulnerability.
B. Impulsivity
C. Macho

**Question 54.**      According to 14 CFR part 107, the responsibility to inspect the small UAS to ensure it is in a safe operating condition rests with the

A. remote pilot-in-command.
B. owner of the small UAS.
C. visual observer.

**Question 55.**      Safety is an important element for a remote pilot to consider prior to operating an unmanned aircraft system. To prevent the final "link" in the accident chain, a remote pilot must consider which methodology?

A. Safety Management System.
B. Risk Management.
C. Crew Resource Management.

**Question 56.**        You are a remote pilot for a co-op energy service provider. You are to use your UA to inspect power lines in a remote area 15 hours away from your home office. After the drive, fatigue impacts your abilities to complete your assignment on time. Fatigue can be recognized

      **A.** as being in an impaired state.
      **B.** by an ability to overcome sleep deprivation.
      **C.** easily by an experienced pilot.

**Question 57.**        A local TV station has hired a remote pilot to operate their small UA to cover news stories. The remote pilot has had multiple near misses with obstacles on the ground and two small UAS accidents. What would be a solution for the news station to improve their operating safety culture?

      **A.** The news station should implement a policy of no more than five crashes/incidents within 6 months.
      **B.** The news station does not need to make any changes; there are times that an accident is unavoidable.
      **C.** The news station should recognize hazardous attitudes and situations and develop standard operating procedures that emphasize safety.

**Question 58.**        (Refer to Figure 22, Area 2.) At Coeur D`Alene which frequency should be used as a Common Traffic Advisory Frequency (CTAF) to monitor airport traffic?

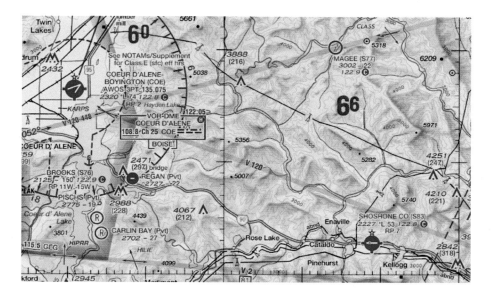

A. 122.05 MHz.

B. 122.8 MHz.

C. 135.075 MHz.

**Question 59.** (Refer to figure 59) What is the frequency for the CTAF at Putnam Co. (OWX) airport in the figure below?

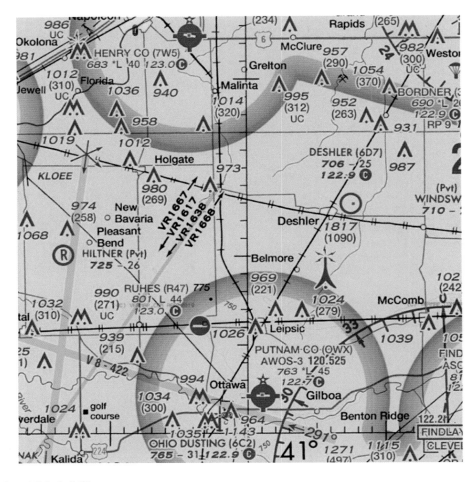

A. 123.0 Mhz

B. 120.525 Mhz

C. 122.7 Mhz

**Question 60.** What class of airspace surrounds Barnes Co (BAC) airport in Figure 26 below?

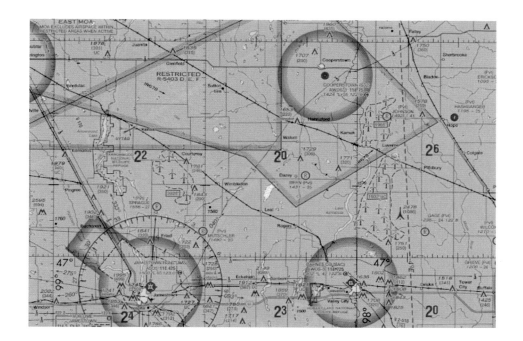

A. Class E with a floor at the surface

B. Class D

C. Class E with a floor of 700 ft above the surface

**Question 1.** C
**Question 2.** A
**Question 3.** A
**Question 4.** C
**Question 5.** B
**Question 6.** C
**Question 7.** B
**Question 8.** B
**Question 9.** B
**Question 10.** A
**Question 11.** B
**Question 12.** A
**Question 13.** A
**Question 14.** B
**Question 15.** A
**Question 16.** B
**Question 17.** A
**Question 18.** A
**Question 19.** A
**Question 20.** A
**Question 21.** C
**Question 22.** C
**Question 23.** A
**Question 24.** B
**Question 25.** B
**Question 26.** B
**Question 27.** A
**Question 28.** C
**Question 29.** A
**Question 30.** C
**Question 31.** A
**Question 32.** A
**Question 33.** B

**Question 34.** C
**Question 35.** A
**Question 36.** B
**Question 37.** C
**Question 38.** A
**Question 39.** C
**Question 40.** B
**Question 41.** C
**Question 42.** B
**Question 43.** C
**Question 44.** B
**Question 45.** C
**Question 46.** B
**Question 47.** A
**Question 48.** B
**Question 49.** C
**Question 50.** C
**Question 51.** B
**Question 52.** B
**Question 53.** C
**Question 54.** A
**Question 55.** C
**Question 56.** A
**Question 57.** C
**Question 58.** B
**Question 59.** C
**Question 60.** C

**Question 1.** (Refer to Figure 21) What is the floor of the Class E airspace surrounding Mercer County Regional airport?

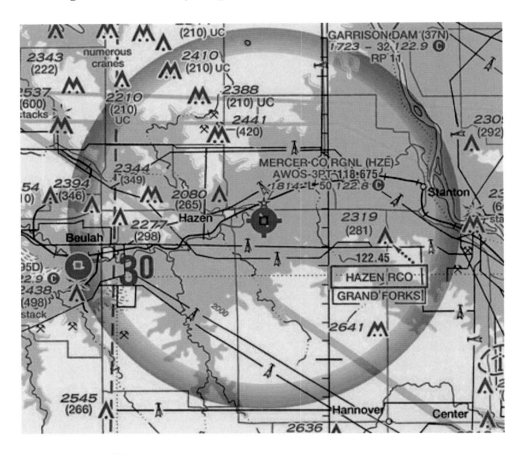

A. 700 feet AGL

B. 700 feet MSL

C. 1,200 feet MSL

**Question 2.** Which of the following is a general operating rule of Part 107?

A. You must only fly in Class G airspace unless you have authorization to fly in controlled airspace

B. Manned aircraft must yield to your drone

C. You can fly your drone at night without prior authorization

**Question 3.** (Refer to Figure 24, area 6) What is the approximate latitude and longitude of Commerce (2F7) airport?

    **A.** 33°18' N - 96°54' W
    **B.** 32°18' N – 95°54 W
    **C.** 33°18' N - 95°54' W

**Question 4.** (Refer to Figure 23) What is the height above the ground of the group of lighted obstacles located near Furman (South of Allendale airport), where the sectional says "antenna farm"?

    **A.** 480 feet MSL
    **B.** 406 feet AGL
    **C.** 342 feet AGL

**Question 5.** Is a licensed Part 107 Pilot allowed to fly a drone in a controlled firing area?

    **A.** Yes
    **B.** Yes, but only with prior authorization
    **C.** No

**Question 6.** Where can a drone pilot access information regarding the existence of a temporary flight restriction (TFR)?

    **A.** Sectional Chart
    **B.** Chart supplement
    **C.** tfr.faa.gov or 1-800-wx-brief

**Question 7.** (Refer to Figure 23, area 2) What is the approximate direction of the runway at the Claxton-Evans County (CWV) airport?

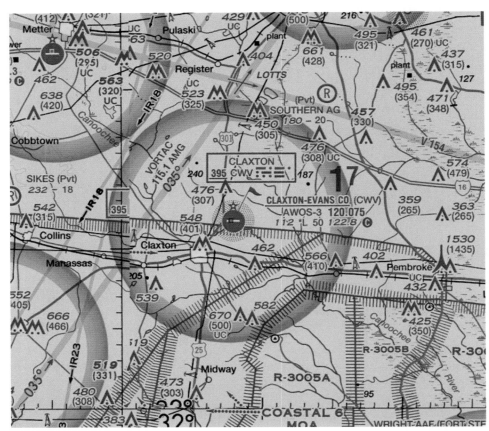

    **A.** North-South
    **B.** East-West

C. Northwest-Southeast

**Question 8.** (Refer to Figure 26, area 2) What is the class of airspace surrounding Cooperstown airport?

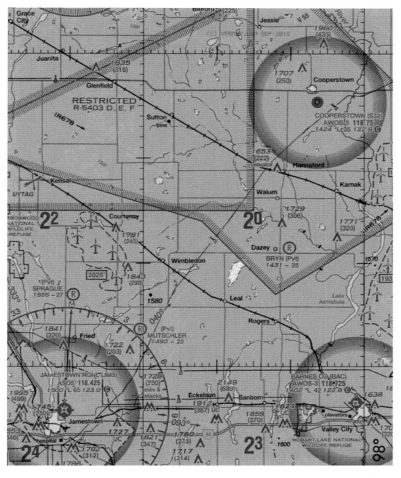

A. Class E
B. Class B
C. Class D

**Question 9.** (Refer to Figure 15) What is the altitude of the overcast layer of clouds on the TAF for KMEM beginning at 2200?

```
KMEM 121720Z 1218/1324 20012KT 5SM HZ BKN030 PROB40 2022 1SM TSRA OVC008CB
    FM2200 33015G20KT P6SM BKN015 OVC025 PROB40 2202 3SM SHRA
    FM0200 35012KT OVC008 PROB40 0205 2SM-RASN BECMG 0608 02008KT BKN012
    BECMG 1310/1312 00000KT 3SM BR SKC TEMPO 1212/1214 1/2SM FG
    FM131600 VRB06KT P6SM SKC=
```

A. 250 AGL

B. 1,500 MSL

C. 2,500AGL


**Question 10.**   When does moisture condense into a form of precipitation?

A. When the dew point is below freezing
B. When the temperature of the air becomes the same as the dew point
C. When the temperature of the air becomes lower very quickly

**Question 11.**   (Refer to Figure 23) What is the CTAF radio frequency for the Allendale County (AOX) airport?

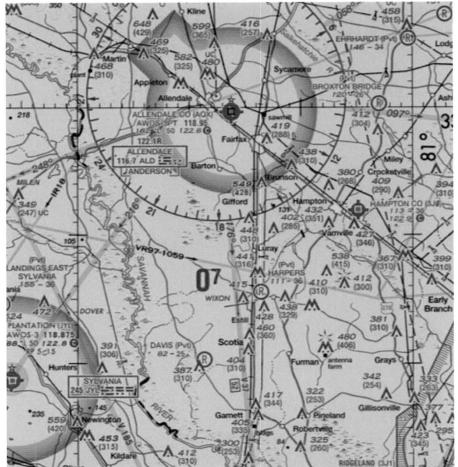

A. 120.975 Mhz
B. 118.95 Mhz
C. 122.8 Mhz

**Question 12.** (Refer to figure 23, area 3) What is the potential flight hazard shown on the sectional map just to the southwest of Ridgeland (3JI) airport?

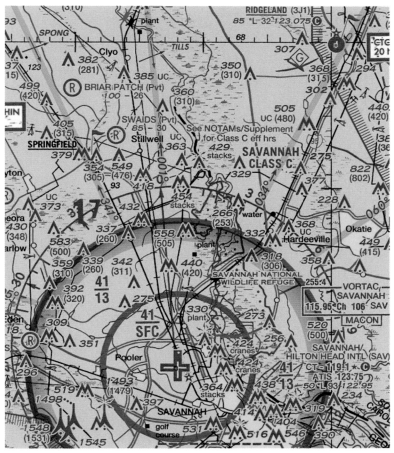

A. Obstruction above 1,000 feet AGL
B. Glider Operations
C. Ultralight Activity

**Question 13.** (Refer to figure 21, area 2) What does the magenta line with perpendicular magenta lines sticking out from it indicate on the sectional map?

A. Prohibited Area
B. Military Operations Area (MOA)
C. Alert Area

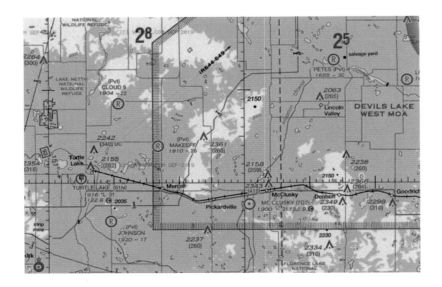

**Question 14.** Do the Part 107 regulations require a commercial drone pilot to use a visual observer when the pilot is using first person viewer googles during drone flight?

    **A.** Yes
    **B.** No
    **C.** Only in controlled airspace

**Question 15.** A drone pilot must report any accident that results in a serious injury to the FAA within:

    **A.** 30 Days
    **B.** 15 Days
    **C.** 10 Days

**Question 16.** A drone pilot with the attitude of "What's the point?" would be indicating which of the following hazardous attitudes?

    **A.** Macho
    **B.** Resignation
    **C.** Impulsivity

**Question 17.** Is a drone pilot able to legally deviate from the Part 107 regulations in response to an emergency?

    **A.** No
    **B.** Yes
    **C.** Yes, but only if there is no visual observer

**Question 18.** (Refer to Figure 2) According to the chart below, what is the load factor on an aircraft that makes a 60 degree turn?

    **A.** 1.414
    **B.** 2.000
    **C.** 2.923

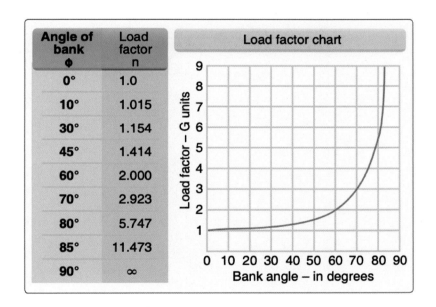

**Question 19.** You are getting ready to fly your drone for a mission and as you are attaching a propeller, find that it has a crack in it. How should you proceed?

    **A.** Dispose of the damaged propeller and replace it with a new one
    **B.** Go ahead and fly today, making sure to replace the propeller before the next flight
    **C.** Just continue to use the cracked propeller

**Question 20.**      What is low-level wind shear?

A. Any wind below 1,000 feet above the ground
B. The force of wind at lower altitudes
C. A sudden, drastic change in wind speed and/or direction


**Question 21.**      What happens when the dew point is the same as the temperature of the air?

A. The air is saturated with moisture and begins to condense in the form of precipitation
B. The moisture in the air freezes
C. Clouds are formed


**Question 22.**      What is the only class of uncontrolled airspace?

A. Class C
B. Class E
C. Class G

**Question 23.** (Refer to Figure 20, area 3) What is the ceiling of the Class D Airspace surrounding Elizabeth Regional airport?

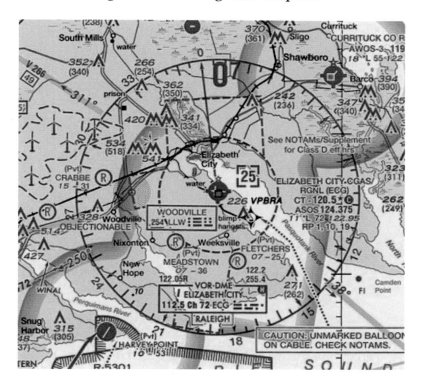

A. 2,500 feet MSL

B. 2,500 feet AGL

C. 4,000 MSL

**Question 24.** (Refer to Figure 20, area 5) What is the height above the ground of the obstacle located at Harbinger on the map.

A. 1,048 feet

B. 1,041 feet

C. 1,000 feet

**Question 25.** (Refer to Figure 12) What is the wind direction and speed at KLAX in the METAR below?

METAR KLAX 121852Z 25004KT 6SM BR SCT007 SCT250 16/15 A2991

A. 250 Degrees at 4 knots

B. 040 Degrees at 25 knots

C. 004 Degrees at 25 knots

**Question 26.**    (Refer to Figure 23, area 3) What does the magenta flag marked "SPRINGFIELD" indicate on the map below?

A. This flag marks the location for a future obstruction that has not yet been built

B. This flag marks the location for power lines running through this location

C. This flag marks the location for a VFR checkpoint

**Question 27.**    What hazardous attitude is being displayed when a drone pilot is ignoring the rules.

A. Anti-authority

B. Resignation

C. Invulnerability

**Question 28.**    Under current Part 107 regulations, how many drones is a Part 107 pilot able to fly at once?

A. One

**B.** Four

**C.** An unlimited number of drones

**Question 29.** (Refer to Figure 25, area 5) What does the number 110/SFC next to the Dallas Fort Worth airport mean in the figure below?

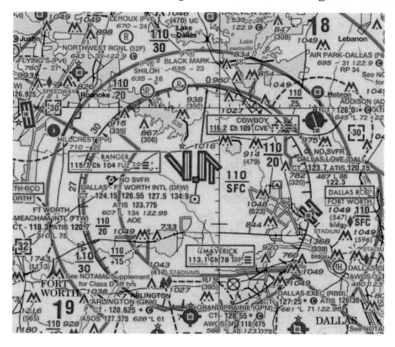

**A.** The highest or lowest altitude that an aircraft can fly in that area

**B.** The altitude in MSL of the runways at the airport

**C.** The floor and ceiling of the airspace surrounding the airport at that location

**Question 30.** You have been asked to fly a mission to inspect a cell phone tower that extends 600 feet above the ground. If you stay within 400 feet of the cell tower, what is the maximum height that you can fly above the ground during your inspection?

**A.** 600 feet AGL

**B.** 1,000 feet AGL

**C.** 400 feet AGL

**Question 31.** When are you legally able to fly a drone for commercial purposes from a moving vehicle?

A. Never

B. Outside of city limits

C. Over sparsely populated areas

**Question 32.**     In what situation would you need to use a visual observer?

A. When the drone pilot is using first person viewer goggles

B. Never

C. Only in controlled airspace

**Question 33.**     Which direction to aircraft typically fly when they are landing?

A. Into the wind

B. With the wind

C. Into a crosswind

**Question 34.**     In a standard airport landing pattern, how will an aircraft typically enter the pattern?

A. On the downwind leg

B. 45 degrees to the downwind leg

C. On the base leg

**Question 35.**     Where would you find information on whether an airport has a part-time tower?

A. Sectional chart

B. NOTAM

C. Chart Supplements

**Question 36.**     What is a NOTAM?

A. Notice of time critical airspace and flight information

B. Notice of bad weather approaching

C. Notice of high levels of air traffic

**Question 37.** (Refer to Figure 26, area 2) What does the magenta C in a circle mean at the Cooperstown airport in the figure below?

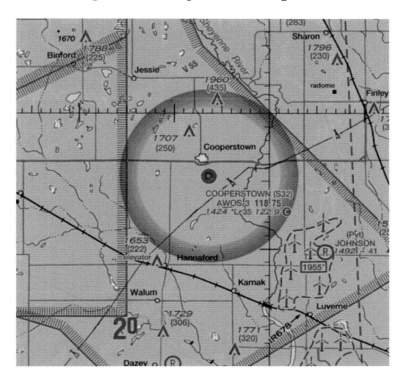

A. This radio frequency is the CTAF or common traffic advisory frequency

B. This radio frequency is the current Unicom

C. That the airport has a control tower

**Question 38.** You have been asked to fly a drone mission to get a better understanding of traffic patterns at a busy intersection in your town. Are you able to complete this mission legally?

A. Yes, so long as you do not fly directly over people

B. No, not in city limits

C. Not without a waiver

**Question 39.** What is the minimum visibility required to be able to operate your drone legally under Part 107?

    **A.** Not less than 5 statute miles
    **B.** Not less than 3 statute miles
    **C.** Not less than 1 statute mile


**Question 40.** What type of clouds can develop into a thunderstorm?

    **A.** Cirrus
    **B.** Altocirrus
    **C.** Cumulus


**Question 41.** Who is ultimately responsible for the safe flight of a drone?

    **A.** The Pilot-in-Command (PIC)
    **B.** The visual observer
    **C.** A local FAA officer


**Question 42.** Which abbreviation on a sectional chart indicates that a radio frequency is used for weather updates?

    **A.** CTAF
    **B.** UNICOM
    **C.** AWOS

**Question 43.** Which direction do the lines of latitude on the earth run?

    **A.** Horizontal
    **B.** Vertical
    **C.** Diagonal


**Question 44.** What is an antidote for hyperventilation?

    **A.** Drink more water

**B.** Slowing the rate of breathing

**C.** Taking time to rest

**Question 45.**     You have been hired to fly a drone mission to photograph progress on a local commercial real estate development. As you are flying, you realize that there is a hospital with a helipad and a helicopter is approaching to land. You have no choice but to fly to 500 feet above the ground. Are you able to legally do this?

**A.** Only one time

**B.** Yes, but you may be asked to report the deviation to the FAA

**C.** No

**Question 46.**     Which of the following event would have a temporary flight restriction surrounding the event?

**A.** A college football game

**B.** A High school football game

**C.** Large indoor event

**Question 47.**     What is the best way to determine your drone's maximum weight limit?

**A.** Test the weight limit to check

**B.** Follow the manufacturer's guidelines

**C.** Use common sense

**Question 48.**     How would a drone be made less stable in flight?

**A.** Weight is added to the drone in a way that hampers controllability

**B.** You land the drone to change a battery

**C.** You change the color of the drone

**Question 49.** You have been hired to fly a drone mission for a local high school event. During your normal pre-flight check it comes to your attention that there is a structural problem with the drone that will affect its ability to fly safely. What is the best course of action.

    **A.** Do nothing and fly anyway
    **B.** Make a temporary fix to the drone
    **C.** Follow manufacturer guidelines and cancel flight if necessary

**Question 50.** Are you able to fly your drone in an area marked as a "Controlled Firing Area"?

    **A.** Yes, these areas typically pose no risk to drone flights
    **B.** No, drone flight is prohibited in a controlled flight area
    **C.** Not without prior approval

**Question 51.**     (Refer to Figure 26, area 4) What is the approximate latitude and longitude of the Jamestown Regional airport in the figure below?

    **A.** 46°55' N - 98° 40' W

    **B.** 47°05' N - 98° 40' W

    **C.** 47°05' N - 99° 40' W

**Question 52.**     What type of airspace surrounds the Plantation (JYL) airport?

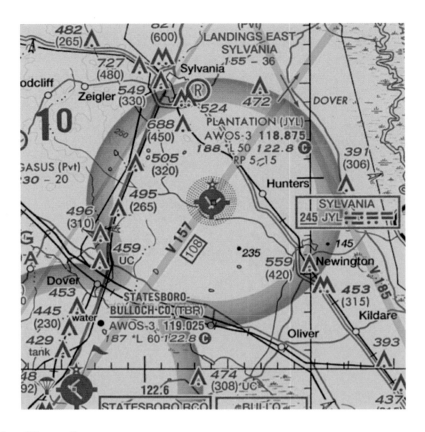

A. Class G

B. Class E

C. Class D

**Question 53.** (Refer to Figure 20, area 3) Does the Elizabeth City Regional airport have a control tower?

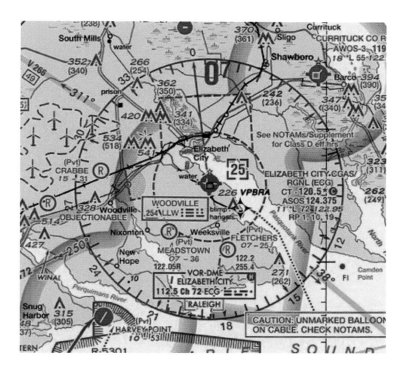

A. Yes
B. No
C. Sometimes

**Question 54.**    What is the maximum speed that you can legally fly your drone?

A. 100 mph
B. 99 mph
C. 80 mph

**Question 55.**    You have been asked to fly a drone mission in a residential neighborhood to get photos and videos of a home that is being sold by a local realtor. The home sits on the edge of Class C airspace and you will need to fly just inside the Class C airspace to get the footage you need. How should you proceed?

A. Just get the footage quickly and no one will know
B. Turn down the mission
C. Request an airspace authorization using the LAANC system or the Drone Zone

**Question 56.**     As a licensed Part 107 pilot, are you able to fly in Class G airspace during the day without requesting a waiver or authorization?

    **A.** Yes, assuming there are no other airspace issues
    **B.** No, you need a waiver to fly during the day
    **C.** No, never

**Question 57.**     For how long is your Part 107 certificate valid before you are required to pass a recurrent exam?

    **A.** 1 year
    **B.** 2 years
    **C.** 5 years

**Question 58.**     The President has flown in to your local airport and there is a TFR in an area where you have been asked to fly a drone mission in airspace that is covered by the TFR. How should you proceed?

    **A.** Fly anyway and stay below 200 feet AGL
    **B.** Re-schedule the mission for a time when the TFR is no in place
    **C.** Request a waiver by call the control tower at your local airport

**Question 59.**     (Refer to Figure 25, area 4) In the figure below, will you need an airspace authorization to complete a drone mission within 3 miles of Decatur (LUD) airport?

    **A.** Yes
    **B.** No, the airspace is uncontrolled below 700 feet AGL
    **C.** Yes, This is Class E airspace

**Question 60.**     Are you able to fly your drone inside airspace marked as a "Prohibited Area"?

    **A.** No, all drone flight is prohibited here

**B.** Yes, with an authorization
**C.** Yes, but only during the day

**Question 1.** A
**Question 2.** A
**Question 3.** C
**Question 4.** B
**Question 5.** A
**Question 6.** C
**Question 7.** B
**Question 8.** A
**Question 9.** C
**Question 10.**    B
**Question 11.**    C
**Question 12.**    B
**Question 13.**    B
**Question 14.**    A
**Question 15.**    C
**Question 16.**    B
**Question 17.**    B
**Question 18.**    B
**Question 19.**    A
**Question 20.**    C
**Question 21.**    A
**Question 22.**    C
**Question 23.**    A
**Question 24.**    B
**Question 25.**    A
**Question 26.**    C
**Question 27.**    A
**Question 28.**    A
**Question 29.**    C
**Question 30.**    B
**Question 31.**    C
**Question 32.**    A
**Question 33.**    A
**Question 34.**    B
**Question 35.**    C

| | |
|---|---|
| **Question 36.** | A |
| **Question 37.** | A |
| **Question 38.** | A |
| **Question 39.** | B |
| **Question 40.** | C |
| **Question 41.** | A |
| **Question 42.** | C |
| **Question 43.** | A |
| **Question 44.** | B |
| **Question 45.** | B |
| **Question 46.** | A |
| **Question 47.** | B |
| **Question 48.** | A |
| **Question 49.** | C |
| **Question 50.** | A |
| **Question 51.** | A |
| **Question 52.** | B |
| **Question 53.** | A |
| **Question 54.** | A |
| **Question 55.** | C |
| **Question 56.** | A |
| **Question 57.** | B |
| **Question 58.** | B |
| **Question 59.** | B |
| **Question 60.** | A |

Made in the USA
Las Vegas, NV
25 October 2022

58150295R00107